ANOTHER TRUE TEXAN SURVIVOR

RON ADAIR

TotalRecall Publications, Inc.
1103 Middlecreek
Friendswood, Texas 77546
281-992-3131 TL
www.TotalRecallPress.com

All rights reserved. Except as permitted under the United States Copyright Act of 1976, No part of this publication may be reproduced, stored in a retrieval system, or transmitted in any form or by any means electronic or mechanical or by photocopying, recording, or otherwise without prior permission of the publisher. Exclusive worldwide content publication / distribution by TotalRecall Publications, Inc.

Copyright © 2021 by: S. R. Adair Jr.
All rights reserved
ISBN: 978-1-64883-038-9
UPC: 6-43977-40389-6

Library of Congress Control Number: 2020942553

FIRST EDITION
1 2 3 4 5 6 7 8 9 10

Judgments as to the suitability of the information herein is the purchaser's responsibility. TotalRecall Publications, Inc. extends no warranties, makes no representations, and assumes no responsibility as to the accuracy or suitability of such information for application to the purchaser's intended purposes or for consequences of its use except as described herein.

The scanning, uploading and distribution of this book via the Internet or via any other means without the permission of the publisher is illegal and punishable by law. Please purchase only authorized electronic editions and do not participate in or encourage electronic piracy of copyrighted materials. Your support of the author's rights is appreciated.

To those who have gone on ahead of me: My Mom, Pops, brother Larry;

Friend from church Mrs. Mary Golden;

Police Officer and good friend Officer John E. Logan, Jr. E.O.W. March 14, 2004;

Mr. David M. Smith, my best friend for over forty years, R.I.P;

To others on this side of life, that have been so supportive in my travels, are;

My best friend today, Mr. Jim Wilson, his wife Pat, and their daughter Janna;

Bro. Steve Hammond;

My sister Lola Rose;

Teresa Rast for help in writing these notes/how our Lord has blessed the life of Ron Adair;

Mr. Homer, and wife Jackie Rushing;

Mr. Michael Rushing;

Mr. "Bubba" Collins, Jr.;

My Forever Friend, Bettie Jane Nelson;

Mrs. Wanda Stewart, Secretary to Mr. David M. Smith;

About the Author

S.R. Adair, Jr (Ron) was born in Houston, Texas and raised in the Alvin and Algoa areas. He was raised to be a hard worker at an early age. In fact, Ron started working with Pops at Adair and Son's Dump Truck and Tractor Work as early as first grade. There will be more of this in the book. He graduated from Santa Fe High School. After school he managed two businesses and was the owner of another before going on active duty in the U.S. Seabees, a division of the Navy dealing with construction and engineering projects. In the Navy he was in Vietnam where he served two tours as Equipment Operator E-5. Since he got out of the military Ron has done a lot to add to his repertoire. One of his favorite things is that he has worked with the Gideons International for 39 years. He also has lead music in church for ten years. So as you will learn and probably already know he has a heart for ministry.

Ron Loves Texas. In fact he loves it so much that he wanted to bring it to Vietnam. With seeds sent to him from home he planted and grew Bluebonnets, which is the state flower of Texas. There it was. In the middle of Vietnam the prettiest blue flowers with trumpet like petals proclaiming to all who saw it the faith of one Ron Adair showing that the God who created this vast universe cared enough to touch the ground with life some 8500 miles from the state Ron called home.

Psalm 139:23-24 says (Search me, O God, and know my heart: try me, and know my thoughts: And see if there be any wicked way in me, and lead me in the way everlasting.) This is what allows Ron to not only know but also show integrity through the God he Loves and Serves so faithfully in everyday life.

Integrity. Now that is a characteristic that is hard to come by in today's world. But it comes as second nature to Ron. When you choose to continue reading this book you will not only know the hard worker he is but also the loving soul he is and that when the Rubber Meets the Road that Integrity, accountability, and true Godly character will become alive again, maybe even through you.

About the Book

In "ANOTHER TRUE TEXAN SURVIVOR" Ron Adair has written from his heart about the many situations, hurts, opportunities, challenges, developments, Worry, FEARS, and "Blessings". These come our way, and how we react, will determine the outcome.

Forward

What do you say when you meet a story teller? Absolutely nothing at all. You just sit back and listen. And listen I did. For nearly twenty years I would sit for sometimes nearly 3 hours fellowshipping with a man who had been everywhere, done everything, and knew everyone. And all I could do is listen, almost mesmerized and hanging on every word he said. Each story somehow was more interesting than the last and made me feel as if I was the one driving the tractor, or the dump truck, or pumping gas, or building roads during the Vietnam War, or cleaning out bays at the carwash, or, well you get the picture. At least I think you will as you read this book.

I met Ron in 2001 at the place of business he managed. You will hear more about this job later in the book. Little did I know our kindred spirit would make him one of my best friends and my closest Christian Brother. If you look in the dictionary of life and look at the name Ron Adair you will see the definition next to the entry that reads: One who gives all, loves all, helps all in the name of his Savior Jesus Christ. And in the stories that make up his life this becomes very evident to anyone who meets him. Ron is uncomfortable speaking of himself and doesn't give unsolicited advice but he finds his comfort zone by asking the Lord to lead him to someone whose life he can make a difference in each day.

Ron Adair has a way with words that keeps you coming back for more. I keep hearing him say "Don't let me beat you up," but I couldn't help it. I was a glutton for punishment when it came to hearing about his life. I have never met a man like him and probably never will again. He loves God, the USA, and the Great State of Texas and will bless your socks off then give you another pair so he can bless them off again. Ok so that part may be a stretch but being around him will make you feel like you are the most blessed person in the world; and you are if you have him as a friend as I would come to know. I have watched Ron not give out of abundance but out of sacrifice to many individuals over the years never hounding for a repayment in kind. He has always had an unquestionable heart of sacrifice and love for others.

When I was growing up there was a brokerage firm with the initials E.F.H. and the tag line was simply when he speaks everyone listens. Well, I can say when Ron Adair is talking just listen. Trust me that will not be hard for you to do. You don't want to miss the wisdom, life lessons, and just shear good ole American know-how that comes from the heart of Ron. As you are reading this book you will hear his mom speaking, his dad's hard work ethic, and the voice of God speaking through Ron's life stories. In short you don't want to miss out meeting "Another True Texan Survivor" like Ron Adair. Just allow your heart, as I and many others through the years have done, to be captivated by this Great Man. I am honored to have him as my friend and Brother in Christ. Blessings in your reading.

By Steve Hammond

Table of Contents:

About the Author iv
About the Book v
Forward vi
Another Texan is Born 1
   Mom's Perspective of Her Life 2
   Ron is Born 6
   Foster Children 10
   Mom's Dump Truck 11
   Graduation, Going Home 13
Adventures in My Early Years 15
   Adair & Sons 18
Alvin Texas, Independent School District 24
   Yellow Jackets Sting Seeeth 24
   Boy Scouts 27
   Salvation 30
Another Teen 39
   Tractor Pulling Truck, Pop, Pop, Pop. 42
   Adair, The Fire Fighter 47
Another Young Adult 58
   Used 1955 Red GMC Dump Truck 60
   Just Another NO, NO! 68
   Another Driver Cannot wait 70
   Another Owner Out of Gas 70
   Another Lost Trailer 70
   Another Veteran 73
   Larry's Texas Weekend 82
   Coming Home To TEXAS 112
General Motors Acceptance Corporation, (GMAC). 113
Another College LeTourneau Institute 115
   C&H Transport Company, Dallas 118
Another Texan Gets Married 119
Best Friend Dave Smith 128
Bells and Dave Smith 134
Another Gideon 156
Another Consulting Opportunity 162

Another Business LADD 168
Another Insurance A.L. Williams 172
    Another Drive Through Backwards 173
Another Challenge MasterGuard 174
Another Marriage / Second Time 175
    AFLAC Insurance Sales 191
CXI Consultant 193
Another Divorce 194
Another Song 195

Another Texan is Born

At my request, my mother wrote about her childhood and early life before and after I was born. Here's our story from her perspective.

My life Ollie Mabel Scott Adair Springer DOB 9-17-1919 today is 8-18-2005

My mother, Maude Isabel Blacklock was a school teacher before she married my father, James Madison Monroe Scott in the early 1900's. They moved to Texas. My dad was an inspector of crossties for the railroad, so we had to follow construction.

I was born in Montgomery County, Texas, on September 17, 1919. I was the youngest of 5 children. My oldest sister, Edith, died after a few months. When I was almost 6, we moved to Alvin, Texas, making the trip in a covered wagon. We camped out the first night by a water tower just across from Aylor's garage and service station. Bud Aylor would be one of our treasured friends and neighbors in Algoa years later.

The next day we settled in the Mustang community south of Alvin. We moved into a large two-story house with the living quarters being on the second story level. The bottom level was completely empty as a basement.

We had apple boxes nailed onto trees for the hens to lay eggs. Occasionally, a chicken snake would be in with the eggs, so I learned to look inside before putting my hand in to reach for eggs!

Mom's Perspective of Her Life

My two sisters went to the small school house about 2 miles from home. The following year, (approx. Summer of 1926) my brother Howard, was due to start school, so we moved to Alvin. About 3 miles west on Davis Bend Road we were offered a house rent free because we had no money for rent.

My two sisters, Essie 12 and Gladys 10, talked to our dad about letting them quit school and getting jobs so we would not have to keep moving. Howard, age 7, could now start school without us having to be on the move. Dad, meanwhile left us there and went on to his next job, which was always out of town. Over the next six years our dad came to visit from time to time, but the times got farther and farther apart.

Essie and Gladys took jobs working in different homes, doing chores to earn money to support us. I started school with a four to five mile walk each way with my brother Howard and the neighbors.

The Lord always provided us with a house rent free, hand-me-down clothes, and garden veggies. My mother was a good seamstress and altered clothes to fit me. When I graduated from Grammar school, I made a pretty white dress from lace curtains given to us!

We walked to church every Sunday morning and night, plus Wednesday night for prayer meetings. When I was Ten years old, our church had a revival service. Our pastor, George W. Springfield, preached like I was the only one there, and at the end of the service the Holy Spirit carried me on air (I don't remember walking) to the altar in front where I knelt down and asked the Lord to be my SAVIOR AND LORD OF MY LIFE!!

Jesus has been my Savior, Guide, Friend, Provider, Peace-giver, you name it, and He has always been there for me. I will be 86 years old this next month, today being August 19, 2005.

My sisters got jobs with the telephone company. We were living just two blocks from school when the new high school building started being built. We walked home each day for lunch, taking a friend to eat with us. Those were the depression years. My sisters were making enough money to finally pay rent, so we moved three miles toward downtown just four blocks from the main part of town. So now, Howard and I had to walk farther to and from school each day.

We finally had electricity, running water, and inside plumbing. It was so nice to have fans for hot weather and a fridge for milk. We had a cow several times before, but this time I learned how to milk it.

As a freshman, I was honored to be the only one in my class to be asked to join the school choir. I had been shy all of my life so our Spanish teacher, Miss Verna Browning, took me under her wings and got me started into our debating class, teaming me with one of my favorite classmates, Alberta McCown.

To my surprise, we went to County meet in Angleton and won third place. Miss Browning was the daughter of one of our local bankers and had traveled worldwide, but was so "down to earth" she never put down any of us or showed any favoritism. Maude Benson was another Gem of a teacher.

Jack O'Neill had a friend who would come to school to pick him up and passed me by as I walked home carrying books. I knew him as Raymond White, who worked in the oilfield and rented a room from an elderly lady who had bought Aylor's Garage and Service Station. He helped work with a tool pusher, so he was nicknamed TOOLIE. She talked him into quitting and going to work for her, running her service station. Jack and Raymond never stopped to flirt or pick up anyone on the road, including me.

All in all, my school years were happy ones. In 1936, Howard graduated and I graduated in 1937, 4th from the top. While I was a senior, I took the job at the telephone company as night operator, so I went to school an hour later than the rest. Back in those days, lots of folks didn't have phones so when a family got a long-distance call, they would pay for a messenger to go to their home with a message to go to the phone office. Guess who walked the miles to get those people word to go to the office? Me or my mother.

After graduation, I got the day time job at the phone company, going to businesses with pay phones. My job was to "rob" the change boxes, count the money and get the manager to sign my copy and give them a receipt. When I got to Mrs. Walton's service station, there was RAYMOND WHITE. I did not know he had left home, following his younger brother Bob.

When he was introduced to others it was as Raymond White. Their dad's name was Andrew White Adair, Sr. The youngest son was Andrew White Adair, Jr., who was nicknamed Tony by Raymond White whose real name was Seth Raymond Adair. It wasn't until after we started dating a year and got serious with each other that he told me his real name. My mother was so sure that I had befriended a crook, she was leery of my getting involved with him, but I had no fears. He started going to church with us and on Sundays when I would be working, he'd go with her. He had never gone to church, so it was all new to him. Weeks passed by and on a Sunday in Sept.1938, he made a public profession of faith and was due for baptism next Sunday on my birthday.

Two days later, however, the company he was working for transferred him to Bunkie, La. Weeks went by but I started making plans to follow him as soon as possible. Our phone system was the old crank type but was being replaced with a more modern dial system. I was asked to stay on and train someone to take my place and was offered a nice wedding OVER THE PHONE AS THE FIRST LONG DISTANCE CALL, plus all sorts of nice gifts from advertisers etc. But I talked to Raymond and we both declined the offer, agreeing that we wanted to be holding hands when we took our oaths. We could not be bought!

On Feb. 7, 1940 I with my suitcase and trunk headed out of Alvin via a bus for Bunkie, La. Seth's landlady picked me up, as Raymond had to work until midnight. The next day he was given 1/2 day off to get married so early the next morning, we headed for Alexandria, La.

After getting the marriage license, we found a nice brick church, went in and asked the colored man cleaning the floors to call the minister as we wanted to get married. He smiled broadly and said "I's he"... then pointed to a church down the road so we ended up in Pineville's Baptist church where Dr. Knight was pastor and ladies in his office were our witnesses.

We grabbed a quick lunch and hurried back to Bunkie so he could go back to work. On his day off, we'd go riding around sight-seeing. Out in the country, we'd stop at the end of a row in a field being plowed and ask where that road would lead us to and usually the farmer would shrink his shoulders or shake his head and say he didn't really know. After staying in his room, renting, I went apartment hunting and found one in the home of the local postmaster and his family, the Couvillions (Coo-ve-yon), a nice French family whose daughter, Martha, was our translator.

That summer a hurricane hit the Gulf Coast, bringing rains and a lot of flooding. Emergency calls went out for phone operators, electricians, etc. Raymond agreed I should offer my help at the phone service. I stayed on after service was restored until that October, when we were transferred back to Texas, moving to Richmond just 2 blocks from the courthouse. We were living there when Pearl Harbor was attacked in 1941.

James Sanders and the welding company he worked for needed extra help and talked Raymond into trying out for welding, which he took to easily. He asked to be called Raymond instead of Seth, which we all did. Jobs were getting farther and farther away, so that fall of '42, he quit and we moved to a two-story duplex at 1569 Telephone Road in Houston. He got a job welding at the Houston Shipyard. I had been praying for a child, and the Lord had finally answered me. I was pregnant when we moved to Houston.

Raymond's brother Tony moved in with us. He walked the streets near our house every afternoon with me so I had company getting my daily exercise. I found a good doctor about 1/2 mile from where we lived. Come to find out, he had moved to Houston from Tyler, Texas. where he had been the doctor for Smith county. He knew Tony and all the Adair family, having treated some of them while most of the kiddoes were growing up when the family lived in Noonday, a small town near Tyler.

Ron is Born

Dr. Homer Gryce really turned out to be a good home delivery doctor, as that was how I wanted it to be for me. On Feb.

9th, three years and one day after we were married, I gave birth to our first son, who weighed 13 and a half pounds. Two hours earlier, our neighbors across the hallway had been over for coffee. Now, Raymond walked over and told them to come see our handsome son, Seth Raymond Jr.

Ollie & Ron

All the time we were expecting him, we had been calling him RONNY for Ronald, the middle name he had chosen instead of Raymond being the oldest of eight children he had never had anything of just his, always having to share. When he saw that little fat white creature, perfect with all ten fingers, ten toes, two eyes, two ears, and one nose, he came to the bed, knelt down beside me and he just burst into tears.

We both thanked God for our gift and promised to raise him

according to the Bible. So, his name is Seth Raymond Adair, Jr., but is still called "Ronny". Valerie and Wesley Adams walked across the hallway, amazed at how fast that baby had arrived. My mother was there, and helped out a lot.

We had prayed for another son, so that in case Raymond did not survive his tour of duty, Ronny would have a playmate. Nine months later, being very pregnant with (hopefully) Ronny's little brother and buddy, I was washing my hair when I had a pain. Knowing how I'd Ronny in such a hurry, I called Al Martin, our good friend who had promised Raymond to get me to the doctor whenever I needed to. I dried my hair with a towel, and off we went to Dr. Merz's clinic. Our second son, another beautiful, big, perfect human being with a full head of dark hair was placed into my arms. My mother named him Lawrence James Adair.

When I brought him home and placed him in the crib built into a side of our bedroom. I went into my mother's house and sat down and hugged Ronny. He went to get a toy and came running back to get me and go see what he had found in the crib a little baby! Oh, how proud he was of that little fellow. They are still very close after all these years, living close to each other and being there for each other.

Raymond had a job in Houston in construction working 7 days straight. Then he was hired by Phillips Petroleum Co. driving a truck, moving drilling rigs from Texas to La. plus delivering parts to and from various places where drilling was going on. He got his forty hours in by Wednesdays, usually, with nothing to do the rest of the week. He bought a good used dump truck, taking orders of different materials to be delivered on Thursdays or Fridays or even Saturdays. A few orders started coming in for delivery sooner, so I got my license to help get the orders onto the truck for him to deliver ASAP. As it got busier, I started making a few deliveries ahead of his getting his forty hours in.

I had always wanted a little red headed girl, so on February 23, 1948, I went to Dr. Merz's clinic to have a beautiful auburn haired perfect little doll. She is grown up now, but still a beautiful person. The boys liked their little sister and really didn't want her to be punished for anything. Time passed quickly, school days for Ronny started and the next year Larry started to school. We started Adair and Sons dump truck and tractor work before the boys ever started school. The boys took to operating any part of equipment needed, being a great help to their dad.

Our church in Algoa was a mission out of South Main Baptist in Houston. Bob Walker and wife Bessie came out from Houston as Bob was our pastor. They would stop by our house for coffee and usually picked up Lola Joyce, our little 18-month doll and we'd not get her back until after church services that night when she and Bessie both cried, not wanting to part.

Roger Neal was born 10:55 am March 29, 1952

Our kiddoes were the greatest ever! Skating became important to the family and our four became champions on skates, playing leap frog over each other, winning races around the rink, doing figure 8's, and playing various games with others. They were competitive in roller hockey with other roller rinks from Houston. When Alvin had a parade, there were several skaters who skated among the floats passing out candy to kiddoes, always ahead of the last horseback riders.

Ronny and Larry were active with scouting, also. I enjoyed taking them and their camping gear out to Camp Mohawk near Liverpool or Camp Karankawa near West Columbia on Friday nights, returning the next afternoon to bring them home. They became Eagle Scouts, earned life guard status plus Ron achieved the God and Country award. Both achieved Order of the Arrow. Ron went on later to become a Scout Master.

Raymond leased a ten-acre piece of land that kept the boys busy in spare times plowing and cultivating. On Saturday nights our boys would bring home an extra boy or two for the weekend. I never knew how many were upstairs asleep until I went up to check things out. One boy, Donald Smith, asked to move in as he had left home and quit school. I had gone to school with his mother and knew his dad so we contacted them. The idea suited them just fine, as he had given them some problems. We let him stay but with our own rules and discipline he would follow or else. He lived with us and helped the boys with their part of the workload.

We bought a dark green new GMC dump truck in 1960 that Ronny drove to school. A few weeks later, Tommy Hooper came home from skating, asked to move in with us, as his mother died when he was just 18 months old and he had been living with his elderly grandmother. After talking it over with the family, he moved in with his shoebox of clothes. Our three boys agreed to take their turns with new clothes, so that was no problem.

Foster Children

A few weeks later, one of our church members asked me to consider taking one of her nephews for a few weeks to see if we could help him overcome his walking in his sleep and having nightmares. So, we got Donald Parker added to our brood. Sure enough, I would hear him upstairs crying. I'd go up and find him scratching the wall of the bedroom and crying. I'd sit him down in my lap, cradle his head on my shoulder and sing him to sleep like a baby, then lay him down on his pallet to sleep the rest of the night. Just a few weeks and he was as normal as the others, sleeping all night with no problems. Prayers and some TLC is all he needed. About a year later he went back to Houston to live with his own mother.

Mom's Dump Truck

The two-story building that housed our boys was built earlier out of tile blocks brought from Houston in my dump truck and constructed by our good neighbor Joe Norris and Whiz White. 4 bedrooms and bath with stair-steps built out of 4"x18"x4' bridge timbers, so they were very sturdy. Downstairs was the two-car garage, room for tools, etc., a large laundry room with two washers, two dryers, and a shower for the boys plus storage shelves underneath the stairs. It really served the purpose well.

We had also contracted with Abe Johnson to build a large truck barn big enough to hold four dump trucks with the concrete floor strong enough to support loaded trucks in at night ready for early deliveries next morning. A welding machine, electric and portable, air compressor, belts of all sizes, storage bins for tires, plows, box-blades, we had it all!!! The kiddoes nick named Raymond POPS which he seemed to like, as a compliment.

In all the years of hauling, I never did wear pants or jeans. Always a nice dress with matching necklace and earrings. Nothing gaudy, so when I had a job delivering a load of gravel to an off-shore drilling rig, I met a barge in Liverpool at the inter-coastal canal pier, drove onto a floating bridge onto the barge, and shut my motor off.

A tug hand asked if I'd like to get out and ride in the tug and sip on a cup of coffee. When we got to the oil rig, I fired up, drove off and up to the rig. I got out of my truck, and all hands stood still and just GAZED at me, not believing what they saw...a WOMAN dressed like she was going to church or somewhere besides a drilling rig off shore!

I smiled, dumped the gravel where the crew showed me, I got my copy signed, and then thanked them for making my day. They were scratching heads as I left the platform and drove back onto the barge and back to LAND!! What a trip!

Years earlier, Pops had showed me how to latch the chains at the bottom of the tailgate of my truck. I could spread shell and I got quite good at doing it after lots of deliveries. When shell was needed the office, workers had a saying: CALL OLLIE BY GOLLY and I would deliver a load of shell to the road. Pops was the best teacher of any piece of equipment made.

After Ronny graduated, he continued to work with Adair and Sons. He started managing a service station in Alvin while still working with Adair and Sons. A year or so later he left that service station to be the Gulf Dealer at Hwy. 6 and 35 intersection. He joined the Seabees Reserve, the construction battalions of the Navy. Because of his knowledge of equipment, he went on active duty March 31, 1966 as E-5, Second Class Petty-officer and was sent to Port Hueneme, California.

When he was ready to be shipped out to Vietnam, he notified us at home and then he asked Lola and me to drive his car home to Texas. Lots and lots of prayers were sent to the Lord in behalf of Ron during his two terms of service in Vietnam and we gave thanks to God for hearing and answering all those prayers. No major injuries, but OH! The memories he will take to his grave are something else.

Meanwhile, Larry graduated and also took a Gulf Dealership on the highway leading into Alvin. Time went by and after Ronny left, Larry up and joined the Air Force, ending up stationed at England Airbase in La.

Lola and I would go visit him and take another (sometimes two) girlfriend with us to pep-up the morale of Larry and some of his buddies. We saw places of interest in that part of Louisiana, Alexandria in particular. Becky Mendenhall was one who made most of all the trips, later marrying Larry and moving to the base.

Ron was offered a job in Huntington as the manager of McDonald's Carwash and Storage for owner, Marvin McDonald, with headquarters in Jasper, Texas. I now volunteer each day Monday through Sunday with time out for church services to each Sunday at McDonald's Carwash and storage, where Ron is Manager. I answer the phone, take messages, help with the unit lists for rentals, the alphabet list, etc. whatever I can do to make things a little easier for Ron. He works 24/7, 7 days a week.

So, here are my memories just a few of them through these 85 years. On September 17, 2005 I will be 86 years old!! WOW!! What a life I can look back on in amazement. God has been so very good to me all of my life!!

Graduation, Going Home

Because HE lives, I can face tomorrow; Because HE lives, all fear is gone. Because I know WHO holds my future, and life is worth the living just because HE lives!! My soul, in sad exile, was out on life's sea, so burdened with sin and distress...until I heard a small voice saying "Make ME your choice, and I entered the haven of REST!!

AAAHAAAHAAAH AMEN

Ollie Age 90

Adventures in My Early Years

My Dad moved Mom and me from 1565 Telephone Road, Houston, (Harris County), Texas. That was where I was born, 10am on Feb. 09, 1943. We moved to 909 Lang St., Alvin, Texas, about thirty miles South of Houston. That is where Mom's Mother owned a large boarding house with a car port on the S. East side. It also had a large wooden porch on three sides of the house. We lived in what appeared to be an Air Stream mobile home, parked under that car port. Grandmother (Maude Scott) was a retired school teacher. I remember the brass teachers bell she had with a black wood handle.

We went to First Baptist Church Alvin. It was just one block South of our home. Mom had learned to play the piano there. I spent many happy days, and hours playing on that large porch, and the many stairs going to so many rooms.

Age 18 months, Equipment Operator

Mom had a Singer sewing machine. I had watched her use it many times. I climbed up onto that machine and turned the wheel that made the needle go up and down. Well, you know how young kids like to put everything into their mouth? Yes, I stuck out my tongue, and ran the needle through it. I was screaming my head off!! Mom came running to me, and got the needle out so I'd be free from that machine. I still have the scars in my tongue. Mom told me years later, that it was all she could do to keep from fainting, when she saw me, and so much blood. Now you know, I have been an equipment operator all my life.

Mom took me with her to a funeral. She left my new baby brother with her mother. While she held me, she commented about all the flowers. She said, "I hope you boys don't wait till I die, to give me flowers". My age was about one year, six months, but I remember that statement, to this day. When we got back home, I picked all the wild flowers that were handy. I put books, pans, and things on top of each other, so I could climb up to our kitchen cabinet. Took one of our jelly drinking glasses, put some water in it, and those flowers. Climbed upon a chair, and put those flowers in that glass, in center of our kitchen table. Mom was as excited about those flowers, as if they had been two dozen Texas Yellow Roses. My brothers, and sister gave flowers to Mom, the rest of her life. We always saw to it, that she had a rose garden nearby.

Years later, we would take trips to Tyler, to visit ken-folk. When we did, I always had an empty cigar box with me. We would visit Uncle Henry, and Aunt Pearl. They lived out in the country, had a mule named Bessie, and a lot of pretty red dirt. I've always loved East Texas with its rolling hills, Pine Forrest, beautiful rivers, and lakes. I would fill my cigar box with some of that pretty red dirt, and put it in Mom's rose garden next to our house, as soon as we got back.

Dad was a welder for the Houston Shipyard. Mom was a telephone operator at the telephone office. My brother Lawrence (Larry) James Adair, was born June 13, 1944, at Dr. Merz's Clinic in Alvin, (Brazoria County). Dad was drafted into the U.S. Navy during WWII. I remember that both of my parents did not know how to swim. Dad received his Honorable Discharge from the Navy, in 1945 from Camp Wallace, (a blimp base) at Hitchcock Naval Air Station. This was about five miles West of Galveston, on highway six, in Galveston County. This blimp base hangar housed six blimps. This was one of the largest wooden buildings in the world. It measured 960 feet long, 328 feet wide, and 200 feet tall.

My folks bought four acres between the Santa Fe Railroad and Hwy. 6, in Algoa, TX., five miles East of Alvin, thirty miles West of Galveston. Algoa population in 1946 was approximately 150 if you count the cows and the chickens. Algoa is in Galveston County, 30 miles West of Galveston Island, on Hwy 6. Alvin is in Brazoria County, 5 miles West of Algoa, and Alvin population in 1946 was approximately 3,500. Alvin is also 30 miles South of Houston, and Houston is in Harris county. Houston population in 1946 was approximately 250,000.

Our home was one of those houses built at Hitchcock Naval Air Station, Camp Wallace. Those Naval servicemen stationed there had no carpentry skills. When this base was closed the buildings were given to servicemen. They just had to pay the moving cost.

Dad had one of these two bed room, wood framed houses delivered to our property and set up on blocks. The ground was low where the house was located. All the doors, windows, walls, floors, ceiling, and even the roof was not square. Hey, the price was right! It had very few wall plugs, and very small closets. Mom had to put wedges of wood under the oven to keep it level. When it rained, we were in mud getting in and out of our home. They put stepping stones down, to get us to the driveway.

Dad worked as an equipment operator for a construction company in Houston. Then he went to work as a truck driver for Phillips (66) Petroleum Company in the large oil fields around Alvin. The area just South of Alvin had a lot of rice fields, and cow pastures. Mustang Road would take you in that direction. Chocolate Bayou, ran through this part of Brazoria, County, so the oil fields in this area were named after that bayou.

Adair & Sons

(A&S) started in 1948 when Dad (Pops) often had his forty hours in by Wednesday, and off work till the next week. With the time on his hands, he bought an "old" Ford truck with a small four-yard, dump bed. He would load that truck by hand, with top soil from the pastures owned by Mr. Ed Lilley, or one of his brothers, B.F., or Babe Lilley. They each had large cow pastures, and a dairy for selling their milk. Using a shovel to load that truck, would take a few hours. Keep in mind, I was helping. When my bucket got full, POPS would empty it into the truck-bed, and I'd load my bucket again, and again. He always had the load sold in advance, and we would deliver it, after dark, before we went home. When we bought our first "old" Ford front-end loader, I thought we were in style, Big Time. We put a large metal box on each side of the blade, in back of this front-end loader. Heavy pieces of steel, and concrete were put in each box to help counter balance the front end, heavy with dirt, or whatever we were loading. The tractor tires in back had water in them for added weight. It was over a mile to the pastures where we would load top soil. Dad would drive the dump truck, and I would drive the front-end loader. Dad tried to hang the front-end loader bucket over the tail-gate of the truck, and pull the tractor with me steering it, but that did not work. The front wheels would shimmy so bad, it was very hard for me to control the tractor. Sometimes we would leave it in the pasture, covered with a heavy canvas tarp. This was JOB # 1 for me, before first grade in school.

Dad would dump a load of dirt next to our house. I would first use a shovel to throw the dirt as far under the edge of the house. When I had a fair-sized pile of dirt under there, I'd crawl under the house. Used a hoe, with a short handle to pull the dirt toward the center. I would move a small pile at a time. It was a very slow go, and a lot of elbow grease, but I would work at it till that pile of dirt was under the house. Dad would bring another load, and under the house it went, with a lot of help from Ronny. I do not know how many loads of dirt were put under our house, or how long I worked on that project, but it was a lot, and for a long time. This is how I earned money to buy my first bicycle.

Adair and Sons attended and took care of the church yard, for First Baptist Church Algoa. We planted Tallow Trees, St. Augustine grass, and gardenia bushes around the church building. I do not remember where my Dad got a bell, but we put it on a fifteen-foot pole, made of 6" iron pipe. Dug the hole for it, and cemented it in the ground, in front of our church. Our Pastor, Bob Walker and his wife Bessie were part of the South Main Baptist Church (SMBC) of Houston support group.

"In 1945, South Main agreed to help restore the building of the Algoa Baptist Church. Four years later, the struggling church in Algoa, Texas signed its property over to South Main. In order to rescue the church, the members of South Main began to hold worship services, Bible studies, and Training Union meetings at Algoa. By 1953, a grateful Algoa Baptist Church was able to purchase the deed back from South Main."

The above "quote" is taken from "THE BUILDING OF A CHURCH" 100 years of South Main. The quote is on page 50 of that SMBC History Book. On the next page (51), shows a picture of South Main's Pastor Dr. E. Hermond Westmoreland (1938-

1971). Just under his picture is this note, "Once upon a time, when the church was young, a visiting preacher sat on the rostrum with Dr. Westmoreland. As the deacons took up the collection, Westmoreland whispered to the visitor, 'Did you know that Cain and Abel are dwelling in unity in this church?' He pointed out that Hiram Cain and Louis Abel were at that moment passing collection plates together. --From 'Library Notes,' May 1956.

```
Sold To _____
Date _____ 19___                    N°  2314
Received From _____
              Adair's Sand and Gravel
         BACKHOE, DUMP TRUCK, MAINTAINER and TRACTOR WORK
Phone 925-3596 -:- Algoa   Phone 585-2272 -:- Alvin   Phone 331-3006 -:- Alvin
                 Rt. 2, Box 560 -:- Alvin, Texas 77511
Sand _____; Topsoil _____; Shell _____; Gravel _____
Fill Dirt _____; Limestone _____; Asst. Road Material _____
Equipment Time _____; Misc. _____
_____
                    Signed _____
```

Adair & Sons work order

Miss Johnnie Green, and Sue Windsor were my Sunday School teachers. They were part of this support team from South Main. They really made the Bible come to life, with stories, and pictures. Another preacher from South Main was Terry Young, he too was very good with Bible stories. Mom would play the piano as we sang beautiful songs like "WERE MARCHING TO ZION". That is still one of my most favorite songs. It seemed strange to me that we would only sing the first, second, and last lines of any song. The words in the "other lines" were GREAT, but were left out "in the interest of time".

Date: _____ № 278

ADAIR & SONS

DUMP TRUCKS • DOZER • LOADER & TRACTOR
MORTAR SAND • BANK SAND • GRAVEL
SHELL • LIMESTONE

RT. 2, BOX 760   ALVIN, TEXAS 77511
337-4851   331-3006   925-3596

Sold To: _____
Street No.: _____
City: _____

Job No. _____

Truck No. _____ Location _____
Start _____ Finish _____

MATERIAL	YARDS	UNIT PRICE	TOTAL
Sand			
Top Soil			
Fill Dirt			
Limestone			
Gravel			

Received by: _____

Adair & Sons work order

Pops was a deacon, and the church treasurer. Mom and my sister Lola would clean and take care of the inside of our church. I remember when our church voted to change the name to FIRST BAPTIST CHURCH OF ALGOA.

In 1952, I too became a new Christian, and was baptised in our church. This was my church home until active duty in the Seabees, March 1966.

We had a LaSalle car, dark green, later on it was replaced by a blue De Sota. My dad had an old jalopy that he rigged-up with a 3-inch pipe coming up out of the hood. He had a quart can of old oil suspended over the motor's exhaust manifold, with a wire that came back through the fire wall and dash. When he wanted to get someone's attention, he would pull on that wire to pour oil onto the hot manifold. That would make a lot of smoke come out of his pipe stuck in the hood. He would make his own smoke screen, going down the highway. He had fun with that. Mom would let me do it once in a great while.

Dad's Mom, Grandma, told me when he got his first car, he was so proud. The next day he drove it into town, later when he got home, he was asked, where is your car. Truth is, he forgot he had one, and walked all the way home. She also told me that one time he came home in it, and was going to park it in their garage. Instead of putting his foot on the brake, he pushed on the gas, and drove it out the back wall.

You need to know; our Mom was a great cook. Thanks to her, I too, know how to cook, (I don't, but I do know how). She would let me help her in our kitchen, making everything, cornbread, biscuits, mashed potatoes (I liked to put in a whole stick of butter). Everything, was great, especially cakes, and pies. The honest truth, she would make twelve, to sixteen pies, and more, at a time. She would make extra pie crust, and cut it in strips, and put them on a cookie pan and, in the oven, to cook, just to let us snack on. When she made a layer cake, and it got cool enough, (after it had the icing on) I always tried to be the one to cut into it first. Why, because when others saw my piece gone, everyone knew Ronny had taken it. How, did they know? I have always liked to be different, to be the exception, to make a difference. Where does anyone start to cut a cake? Any cake? Some corner, right (?), or if it is round, slice it from the center, and take out a wedge from that first cut, and the side of that cut. When you see a layer cake that Ronny got to first, it will have a two-inch square hole in the center of it.

We built a heavy, large, two wheeled tractor trailer. We used a heavy front-end axle, that came from a large truck. We used this trailer to move our second, "old" Ford tractor home. The second tractor was used to level dirt, plow, disk, brush-hog mowing, or digging post holes, all types of attachments, that used a three-point hookup. We had built a truck shed, and tractor shed. Our first work shop, was bought from Sears and Roebuck. They delivered, and set it up in one day. We traded that first Ford dump truck in for a larger, and better truck. This truck had a green cab, and we had an eight-yard dump bed put on it. Clem's Paint & Body Shop in Alvin, painted that dump bed bright yellow. The Adair and Sons, (A&S) dump truck and tractor work, were growing in more ways than one.

Alvin Texas, Independent School District

My first day in school in Alvin, Texas, (the Yellow Jackets), was a day to remember. The teacher told us to raise our hand, and say present, or here, when she called our name. Ronny Adair is my name, and at that time I had no clue that an alphabetical listing was being used.

Yellow Jackets Sting Seeeth

The first name she called was Seeth,... Seeth..., no one was answering "here", and I started chuckling. The teacher calls again Seeth, and then calls Adair..., I was in shock. Ever so slowly, I raised my hand, as I slumped lower down in my seat, and said "here". That was a hard pill for me to take. When I got home, I asked Mom, what is this Seeth bit, for my name. She said get the Bible, and she showed me the name of Adam and Eve's third son was Seth. It means replacement. I'm named after my father, Seth Raymond Adair, Sr., I'm Jr., and all my life (six years), Ronny Adair was the only name I knew.

It was almost a mile walk from our home, in Galveston County, to the Brazoria County line, and road going South from Hwy 6. That is where I caught the Alvin Bus to go to school. It came from the South, going through Floraville, and crossing the Santa Fe Railroad to turn West, onto highway six. From this point, Alvin was about four miles. This was in all kinds of weather. The Santa Fe ISD, had a bus that came by our house on Hwy 6. Before starting the second grade, Mom made it possible for me to board this bus, and go to Santa Fe Elementary, in Arcadia, Texas, just three miles East. Mrs. Watts drove that bus,

#7, and was a great lady. She drove trucks during World War II.

Age 7

While in second grade I learned to ride a bicycle belonging to my cousin Dennis. Wanting and getting my own bike, was made possible, by putting dirt under our house. It helped me start my own line of credit for a new Western Flyer bike at our Western Auto Store in Alvin. Later I bought my first tool box, Wizard tools, and Silverton Radio, all on my good credit, and about age 7.

One morning, a salesman knocked on our front door. Larry was playing on the floor in the living room. He got up and ran toward the door, to see who was there. He stepped on the lid of a metal can that was part of his toys. It had been one of those cans you take the key fastened on one end, that is on the top of the can, to attach, then you turn it, and it rolls the metal seal from around the can. That leaves a smooth edge on the can, because that is the way the can is made. What is not smooth, is the top, that should be thrown away, because it is very sharp. Larry stepped on that sharp lid, going to the door. Mom said it almost cut his big toe off. I remember cleaning up a big puddle of blood off the floor. Dr. Merz here we come.

Age 8

In 1951, third grade, one day before classes started, I was swinging. Going so high, trying to go higher, than this friend swinging next to me. His name was Money Jones. That's right, perhaps he was born late in December. He might have been a tax advantage to his parents. You know, another deductible on their tax return. He lived just down highway six from our home. He was swinging higher, and higher. The higher we swung the more slack would get in the chains. We would drop in our seats till that slack was taken up. When that happens, you get a hard jolt of gravity trying to pull you down to earth. He won, when I fell out of the swing, and hurt my arm. It was really hurting a lot. I would not cry, but all I could do was hold my right arm in so much pain. A girl friend, Millie Hoyland, told our teacher what had happened, and Mom was called to come get me. She took me to Dr. Merz's Clinic in Alvin. The bone had a hair-line crack, so he put my arm in a plaster cast for a while. This same year I had a near death experience while on my bike and hit by a car.

(See A.N.D.E. Volume 2 for details.)

It was about this time that we had Mr. Abe Johnson build our large truck barn. It had a solid concrete floor, and was high enough in the center for a dump truck with an eight-yard bed, to be raised up, so it could be worked on, and not touch the roof.

It was long enough to hold four dump trucks, and a pick-up truck. We had a large air-compressor, welding machines, several large work benches, tire tools, to fix flats, and a lot of iron on shelves, or racks. We had, angle iron, round rod, flat bar, in most any size, and a lot of scrap metal.

We went to a new Oliver Tractor Supply store on FM 517 near Dickenson, TX to buy a new tandem disk. We brought our Ford tractor to hook up to it and take it home. We were told that our tractor was to small, and could not handle it. We hooked up to the new disk, and when we tried to lift it, the two front wheels on our tractor came off the ground and into the air. WOW, it was a heavy disk. So we bought an Oliver, Super 55 tractor from them, that would handle it. Oliver tractors are painted green. Our school colors were green and gold, so when we bought new trucks they were usually green, and we would paint the dump-bed yellow.

Boy Scouts

Age 9

Another Boy Scout at age 9 in 1952 in Algoa Troop 23. Mom had made it possible for the boys, (Larry, and me), to join, and be involved with other guys, training, and teaching us all the things we would need to learn about scouting and life.

Mr. Cecil Williams was Scout Master, and a neighbor. His two sons, Donald and David, also in our troop, were several years ahead of me. Others in our troop, and all older than I was, were Tom Summeral, John Mendenhall, Charles Van Dyke, James Mittlested, Otto and Ben Rezek.

Still more my age joined when I did. They were Darrell Mittlested, his twin brother Donald, James Kitchell, Ted Almendarez, Sammy Cheshire, Elmer (Spider) Webb Jr., & Larry Adair (my younger brother), Butch Unger, and Paul Van Dyke. Mr. Webb started working as Assistant Scout Master with Mr. Williams, and we had quite an active and "involved" troop.

Our sponsor was, the Ladies Home Demonstration Club. They had a fair-size building, and had a portion of it available to our Boy Scout Troop 23. The Scouts had a snake collection in glass jars with formaldehyde. That collection was kept out of sight by a curtain across the front of those shelves.

Learning how to swim, canoe, was so very rewarding. These skills, and more, proved so beneficial throughout my life. Scouting was a welcomed break from the activities of Adair and Sons (A&S), school, and church.

Given the opportunity, we earned merit badges, from projects like archery, tying knots, build a fire, Safety, First Aid, Home Repairs, Corn Farming, Swimming, Life Guard, Canoeing (over fifty miles), just to name a few. Scouting was so helpful in learning how to work as a team, being a leader, and helping the younger scouts to learn by our example.

Ron's Boy Scout Awards:
Eagle, God and Country, and Silver Eagle

On one training exercise, Donald Williams, was teaching us how to properly use an axe to cut limbs from a fallen tree. At some point the axe bounced off a limb and cut into his leg. It was a bad cut, blood was shooting out, from a cut artery, and we learned how to properly apply direct pressure, and got him to a doctor. Later on we were shown how to clean, and care for that cut. Donald was always one of my favorite leaders in our troop.

On one camp out he drove into town to get a few supplies, and asked me to come with him. We stopped at the DQ, (TX Dairy Queen, ice cream place), and he told them to give me the biggest ice cream cone they had. WOW, it was the tallest one I had ever seen, and good to the last drop. He was my hero.

Each year, when we would celebrate the Scouts birthday, we would go to church as a troop, together in our uniforms. We took turns going to different churches that each family went to. The Mittlested boys, were Church of Christ. Most of us were Baptist.

Paul and his older brother Charles were Catholic. We all earned the high Eagle Scout Award, and later, the even higher Silver Eagle. I was the only scout in our troop to ever earn the God and Country award. That took a lot of learning scripture, understanding the Christian faith, along with how, and why to pray.

Algoa Explorer Post 423 L to R is Darrell Mittelsted Ron Adair, Sammie Chesshir, Jack Unger, Elmer Webb, Jr., Donald Mittelsted, Jim Kitchell, and Larry Adair; all received the Eagle and the Silver Eagle award.

One Summer, a nearby neighbor family lost their older son, about age 9. He drowned in a large rice canal. The family ask the scout troop to be Paul-bearers at the Catholic Funeral. I was one of those asked to serve.

Ron in first roe, second from left, Next to Ron is the Life guard instructor, then Donald and Darrell Mittelsted

Salvation

We went to church every Sunday, morning and night. That was a day of rest. Mom could read me like a book. For years, I had been asking her questions about the bible, and some of the stories we were taught in Sunday School. I had questions for our pastor, teachers, and God. Why did Jesus love me so much, that He would die, for me, and for everyone that believed in Him? I knew in my heart that Ronny Adair should trust in Jesus, to save me before it was ever lasting too late.

Mom was going into Alvin, to get parts needed for repairs to a truck, and I asked to ride along. That was a ride where normally we would be talking to each other. She drove, and I just rode, not saying a word. I was thinking very hard about my decision to accept Christ. Mom pulled in front of Roark's Auto Supply, and I told her we needed to talk. She let me talk about my decision to know that I was accepting Christ as my personal savior. I wanted to live for Him, and trust my life to follow our Lord Jesus Christ. She led me in a sinner's prayer, and when we hugged, I could not wait to run in and tell my good friend Ronny Roark. He was just a year or so older than me. All the Roark's were happy for me, with smiles on every face. My brother Larry, and I talked about my decision. He said he felt the same way. The next Sunday we both came forward, and told our pastor publicly, and joined the First Baptist Church of Algoa. We were both baptized soon after that. Our Lord has had His hand on my life, all my life. I have always tried to be thankful for His every blessing.

Age 10

At age 10 we were working on a foundation, and building a two-story garage apartment for the Adair boys. Roger Neal Adair was our youngest brother, now about a year old. Ok, I've saved the best for last, we have a sister, Lola Joyce Adair. At this time, she is about five years of age, about five years younger than me, and Roger is ten years younger. Mom has had her own International dump truck with green cab, and 8-yard, yellow dump-bed, for a few years now. She was helping with deliveries, while Dad was at his regular job for Phillips 66, driving a truck. Mr. George Barrel, was Dad's helper, and rode together in the company truck. Mr. Barrel had his own water well drilling service, that he did after he was off work. They made a good team, and worked well together.

Mom is using her truck to make trips into Houston, where we were getting the concrete blocks for our building project. We unloaded her truck by hand, and Larry would help me push our little red wagon full of these blocks to the place where they were needed. Working on this project, and helping Pops set heavy concrete culverts for driveways hurt my back. Many trips were made going to the Chiropractor for treatments over the years. My first treatments, were as I remember, about one, or two a week. This would be repeated till the ache and pain stopped, probably about a month. Go back again, a year or so later, this went on till about age 16.

Age 11

About my age 11 we were coming home from church one Sunday when we had a visiting preacher going to eat lunch with the Adair's. Mom and Dad had already left church, I waited to ride with the preacher, and show him where we lived. As we got near our home, the traffic had stopped from both directions in front of our driveway. There were several cars stopped in front of us, and I'm wondering why this man is standing in the road holding us up.

Here comes little brother, age 2, pushing a toy dump truck from our driveway, into the highway, and going across the road. I jumped out, and ran to get Roger, and his truck, and carried him back into our yard, as I gave a sincere, THANK YOU to the man that had held up traffic for Rogers safety. We had a great lunch, always did, with Mom's cooking.

We had a wood picnic table under a willow tree in back of our house. We also had a cold water melon, in the Fridge. We, decided it was time to eat it, while Mom, and Pops were gone. Larry brought it out to the table, while I went after the knife to cut it open. The right knife, I thought, would be the new machete

Pops, and I had just made. We had made it from an old broken saw blade. It was very sharp, and had a nice new wood handle. It cut right through that melon, like a hot knife through butter. There was a problem, the knife stopped when it hit the wood picnic table, my hand did not stop when the knife did. My right hand slipped off the handle, and onto the blade, down to the melon. My hand had a two-inch cut, half an inch deep, and I saw the white meat split in my hand. Larry got the water hose, and washed off the melon. I washed off my hand with water, then hydrogen peroxide, and wrapped it in a wash cloth. All were sworn to secrecy, we just told Mom I had cut my hand. She never saw it, and I did not go to the doctor for stitches. I just kept it clean, and a good bandage on it, while it healed up. The fine line scar is still seen today.

We got our two-story garage apartment built, with a little help from Joe Norris, a neighbor that was a great carpenter, and friend. He and his wife Birdell, had a daughter Ruth and a son, Joe Jr., both several years older than me. They lived just a block away at the corner of Thompson Rd. and Hwy. 6. Joe had helped put in the windows, the stairs, the frame work for the walls, the hardwood floors, and all the electrical needed for both upstairs and ground floor.

The building had two parking spaces in the back, or Southend, with doors that slid out and down. Room to walk between the vehicles, and around them with the doors down. Under the very strong and heavy staircase, was shelves that held Mom's canning goods. To the front Mom had two washing machines, and two large close dryers. We had a work bench on the wall by the stairs. A large shower stall was on the far end, and near a door leading outside to our truck barn. Joe had put in two large windows facing the front and highway six, so Mom could see the world driving by while washing, and drying clothes.

This was a good addition to the Adair house hold. Larry and I earned more merit badges on this project. We learned about home repairs, electrical, plumbing, welding, carpentry, roofing, masonry, and cement work. We did learn a little more about landscaping, and dirt work. We had new neighbors, Mr. Elmer Webb, and his wife Edith, move into our area. He was a brick mason by trade, and they had a son Elmer, Jr. nicknamed "Spider", and a younger daughter. They hired Adair & Sons, to put in their driveway, build up the place for their mobile home, and put in a septic system. They told us they wanted to build a skating rink, and put in a go-cart track. Pops told them, "we can help with all of that."

Remember Mr. Cecil Williams, the Boy Scout Master? His wife, Margaret, is a sister to Mrs. Edith Webb. Cecil is a carpenter, and helped build this skating rink with maple hardwood floors. A&S got busy, and put in the driveway, and hauled in fill dirt, and fill sand for a pad to put the mobile home on. Built the septic systems for their home, and another for the rink. The driveway and large parking area for the rink, and go cart track was a pleasure to work on. Everyone was anxiously waiting for the opening day. It went over big time, started out with a lot of local support. As the word got out to neighboring cities, they came to the Algoa Skating Rink, and go-cart track, too. Larry and I learned how to skate, about a year earlier. Arcadia's Rungie Park, had a building with a concrete floor, and clamp on skates you could rent. Mom would take us and watch, or come back later to pick us up. I hated those clamp on skates, because every time you fell, the skate would come off your shoe. You had to use the "key" they issued you, to put your skates back on. We fell a lot, but we did learn how to skate without falling as often.

Mr. and Mrs. Webb took a liking to everyone, and they were loved by all. They rented out shoe skates, what a great difference those were especially on their hardwood floor made of maple. They sold new shoe skates, so the Adair kids got some on order pronto. I had my first pair about a year, and then bought a second pair with what Mr. Webb called side walk wheels. They were made with a softer kind of material, that actually held up better on the sidewalk, streets, and roads. The Adair's wore out several sets of wheels on that rink. Spider joined our Boy Scout Troop 23, and became a real buddy to us all. He had a hair lip, and slurred speech, and his mouth slobbered all the time as he tried to talk. He handled himself well, and as folks got to know him he wasn't hard to understand at all.

His Mom Edith was visiting with another sister in Alvin, and they all drove to Pearland, just ten miles up the road. They were crossing a railroad track and got hit by a train. Edith, and son Spider, survived, but Spider's younger sister was killed. Edith's sister, and two of her children were killed also. Edith was in the hospital a long time, and was told she would never walk again. A few years later, she was back on roller skates, and walking as normal as anyone. Sometimes she wore shorts skating, and you could see the scars on both legs where they put the rods, and pins in. She had a great loving spirit about her. Spider took the accident hard, and felt that it should have been him that was killed, not his sister. She had no physical problems, like he had. Later on, one of the young ladies that came from Alvin to skate, fell in love with Spider. They got married and started their own family.

Age 12

Around my age 12, the Adair & Son's were getting more equipment to work with. One new International 450 diesel, front-end loader, with a half yard bucket. Dad felt it need an upgrade on the bucket, it lacked "bite", so we welded on some teeth. These teeth were made from old stainless steel sucker rod from the oil patch. That tractor was a true work horse. We had that tractor for a year or so, when Mom came to me while I was on it going to put fuel in it. She was mad, angry at me and told me to come off that tractor right now. I asked what the problem was about, and she told me about something that I knew Larry had done. She thought I had done whatever it was. I told her I was not coming off this tractor to get a whipping, for what I did not do. That shocked her and me too. She felt like she was losing her authority over me, and started crying.

I remembered Dad making Mom cry once when he used to drink beer, about my age 2. That was the only time I remember Mom crying till now. When she started crying, I could not get off that tractor fast enough. I begged her to whip me. I did not want to do anything to hurt my Mom like that. We both cried and loved each other thru that experience.

Another addition to our fleet was another new Massey-Ferguson tractor. This one we all fell in love with. It was a yellow, 203 diesel, with power steering, and three point hook-up like all our other tractors had. With this one we bought a new "box-blade" that put all our other blades to shame. This one had ripper teeth that you could let down to tear up the ground. This was a time saving tool like we had never had, or even seen before. Another great advantage, was when pushing backwards with this blade, it had a floating blade on the back side that would lock in place to scrape with more force going backward. The blade was boxed in, that kept material, dirt, shell, or whatever we were working with, from drifting out on both ends of the blade. That was one fantastic, outstanding piece of equipment. That tractor came in so handy, and did such a great job, helping us get the job done, better and faster. That was a win, win situation, for us and the customer we were working for. Soon we went back and bought another 203 diesel, with another new box blade, just like the first one. Those were two real work horses, and Larry and I were operating them so smoothly, they were a real pleasure to be on.

One job we had, was helping to build a new cafeteria for the Monsanto Chemical Plant in the Chocolate Bayou Field, Southwest of Galveston about forty miles. Adair & Sons, with Mom's help, had hauled in fill sand for the new foundation. I was operating one of the 203 diesel tractors, with that great box blade, putting the finishing touches to leveling the fill-sand to a specific grade for the cement contractor. Just outside the forms for the building was a big, beautiful tan, wall tent. One end was open with the flaps back, and you could see it was set up with a lot of folding chairs, but no one around. Now, all of a sudden I hear sirens, see a lot of motor cycle cops, vans with emergency lights flashing, and they pull right up to my work space, and stop. I'm pushing, and pulling fill sand ever so carefully to meet the needed grade-level. A lot of important people just came into my work zone, and I have no clue why, but I'm fixing to find out. One very important looking man comes to the edge of my work area, and motions to me to come to him. Ok, I go over, shut off my tractor, and ask how I can help. He tells me, "son, I don't know what they pay you for your work, but Governor Conley, is trying to speak to this building dedication in side of that tent. He is having a hard time trying to talk louder than your tractor. We will pay you three times your rate, just to stop for thirty minutes or so". Ok; asked, and answered. I took a break.

Back home, Dad was working on our heavy tractor trailer. Getting a part moved by hitting a large heavy cold chisel, (it was called a cold chisel, because it was not pointed on the end, just flat), with a sledge hammer. I was holding the chisel for him to hit. He was swinging hard, and hitting it with a lot of force. I trusted Dad. The chisel had mushroomed, where he was hitting it.

On one of those hits, I felt a sting in my left leg, and put the chisel down, and touched my blue jeans, where I felt the pain. He asked what's wrong as he saw me touch my leg. Blood covered my pants, and he told me to pull your pants down. A piece of that metal chisel had went into my leg, making a half inch cut where it hit me. Dad always carried a small screw driver clipped in his shirt pocket, with a small magnet on top. He took that magnet and probed in that cut but did not feel anything. He told Mom to take me to see Dr. Merz, and get it out. When the doctor saw me, and did some more probing, he told us that it might have gone to the bone. He assured us, that where ever it was in my leg that my body would grow a protective coating covering it completely. He said as I got older, that it might work its way to the surface, and just be a small bump under the skin. If, and when that happens, he said, it could easily be removed, or not. Just keep the cut clean, and let it heal. That piece of metal is still there, and I'm still going.

Another Teen

Age 13 Roger Operating A Tractor

When I was about age 13, Roger was three, and had been on every piece of equipment we had, riding with Dad, Larry, or me, from time to time. I felt it was time for the younger Adair's to step up, and help. Remember the Oliver Super 55 tractor with that tandem disk? Yes, I did, put Roger on that tractor by him-self, operating it like a real Pro. I had him disking, less than the length of a football field, which is 100 yards, and headed toward the back of our house. This area was at the base of the Santa Fe Railroad, that we kept mowed, or disked to keep the weeds down on the back side of our four acres. So he is disking slowly, toward the back of our house. I ran ahead of him, and called Mom to come see something special from the back porch. She came out, saw Roger on that Oliver pulling that disk, and to say she started getting very concerned, would be putting it lightly. She said, "he's going to get killed, what were you thinking?" Then she said he is going to hit that utility pole..., she was right, he was heading straight toward that large pole. I simply said, relax, and watch, I too had no idea what he would do. What I did know, was that he had enough experience to not panic. I had that tractor in the lower range of gears, it had two neutrals, and he was in the slower speed. The worst case senario, I knew that the heavy A frame ("A" for Adair), bumper would only hold the tractor in place, if he did let it hit the pole. The driving wheels would keep on turning, but ever so slowly turn in place, in one spot on the ground, till I could go rescue him. Now, that did not happen. What did happen, as I had told Mom to relax, and watch. He got closer, and closer to that pole. Six feet, before bumping into that pole, he reached out to the kill switch, and simply turned the motor off, and the tractor comes to "a putt, putt, stop". I turned to Mom with all the confidence I felt, and said, SEE, he knows what to do. Mom just turned and went back inside the house. Probably thanking our guarding angles, for watching over us.

Another addition to our work horses, was a used yellow Gallion Motor Grader, or commonly called a maintainer. It is a piece of heavy equipment designed to scrape along the ground with two front tires, and the blade is in front of the four rear tires in tandem. The operator stands, or sits, in front of the motor, moving the long, large, blade that can move dirt, or material to the left, or right, with the controls that move the round turntable just above the blade. It can move dirt to the center of a would be road, or runway, for an air-plane. It can be used to clean out a ditch along a road way. I started operating this machine on several jobs. The first job, was at the Alvin train depot, downtown, on business highway 35, and the Santa Fe Railroad. I was about age13. We soon had a second maintainer, it was an Allis-Chambers. Built, and looked the same, just a different manufacturer. Both did the same job, built roads, landing strips for those who had private planes, and the land to build a runway, or landing field. We built one, on the other side of the railroad tracks from our home, for a neighbor that owned a chemical company in Pearland, TX. Another work horse, was a scraper, painted red, with the three point hook-up, but only had two points, to hook-up. Any one of our tractors with the three point hook-up could pull, and operate it. The tractor pulling this scraper would lower the unit to the ground and it would did into the earth and fill the bowl as it is drug along the ground. It had two rear tires to carry the load, when the operator raised it. Then hauled it to a desired dumping spot. The operator could pull a rope, and release the latch holding the bowl of dirt, and dump it in a pile, or let it catch in the spread position, to let the dirt come out in a level bed for filling in a low area. There are larger "scrapers" that have their own motor, power train, and a one-man operator, type of machine. Some scrapers have two engines, one in front, and another behind the bowl to help push the machine, still using only one operator. Adair & Sons never had one that large. However, I did operate both while in the military, and later helping to build Cooper Lake, in East Texas.

Perhaps this would be a good time to explain some of the day-to-day activity we went thru. Yes, we started out with family doing it all, then found it helpful to get more help to get more done, and ring the cash register more often. We made several improvements, as we needed to better communicate. We first bought CB Radio's. They were a tremendous help, but had their limitations, due to distance, weather, static or interference. As we grew, and had more jobs going in different places, we got an upgrade, to Motorola Radio's in all our trucks, and cars. This solved a lot of problems. We had hired truck drivers, equipment operators, mechanics, laborers, dispatchers, bookkeepers, and still hired a lot of things done. We used Clem's paint and body works in Alvin to do work on vehicles as needed. We used Brothers, radiator shop just East of Alvin, on Hwy 6. We had charge accounts for most any need in a fifty-mile radius of Alvin. You get the drift here? Every day was different, like Roger on that tractor at age 3. We just never know, one day to the next how this week will end. When you work for the public, you deal with every kind of person.

We had a dump truck driver not show up at the end of the day. We started to report the truck stolen, but waited till the next morning. He gets to work, and we ask him, where is your truck? He responds, "Oh, it had a flat so I caught a ride home. "He left the keys in the truck, and told us where he left it. This was before we had two way radio's. His services where no longer needed.

We had learned to teach all the workers to watch out, especially on private property for over head power lines, to ask where the septic tank was, and the field lines if we were delivering a heavy load of dirt, gravel or just getting off the drive way, for any reason. Ask, to be certain, so we do not drop off into a septic tank, or soft field line. This happened so many times, we bought our own wench truck, to get our trucks out, and fix the mess, we made. We bought a heavy, large rear wheel used Oliver rice farm tractor, just to pull our trucks and equipment out when, or where ever they got stuck, loaded, or not.

Tractor Pulling Truck, Pop, Pop, Pop. . .

Mom was making a delivery of top soil, in Algoa, to one of the Moore brothers, and she got stuck. Mr. Moore told her, not a problem, I'll get my tractor, and pull you out. Do you have a tow chain? He asked. While she was telling him yes, I got out, and pulled the chain from our tool box. Hooked it to the front of our truck, and waited for him to come with his tractor. I told Mom, I do not think his tractor is going to be able to do the job. Here he comes with this John Deer tractor that sounds like it is on its last day in this world. He backs up to our truck, and I hook the chain to his tow bar. He takes the slack out of the chain, and slowly tries to pull forward. I look at Mom behind the wheel of our truck, as she has our truck in "Grandma", that is what you call first gear, and the truck wheels start to turn ever so slowly. Mr. Moore's tractor is ever so slowly pulling the motor RPM's (revolutions per minute), down lower, and lower, and I'm expecting the tractor motor to just die, and stop. Its motor sounds like this...as he drove it to our truck, and backed up. "Pop, pop, pop, pop, pop, just kept popping, to even take the slack out of the chain. Well now this popping is getting slower, and the time between pops is driving me crazy. I'm thinking, why waist our time, let's call for help. Well it continues... pop.... pop..... pop.......... pop........ pop......... pop............. pop............. pop................., and blow me down, our truck is starting to move ever so slowly, but it does keep moving forward. That tractor started getting the pops closer together, and it pulled Mom's truck free from being stuck. Unbelievable, as I told Mom, and looked at Mr. Moore, as he just smiled with a grin. I took the tow chain, from his tractor, and thanked him. Then put the chain back in our tool box. Mom and I were happy campers. Later on, when I had a chance, to tell Pops, about our experience. He simply told me that the John Deer that pulled Mom out, was known as a "Popping Johnny", because the engine only has one cylinder. I had never heard of a one cylinder motor. Most all motors have at least two, four, six, or eight cylinders to get the job done. That was one strong farm tractor. I remembered laying in bed at night and hearing these tractors plowing in fields at night. I thought they were about to die, and needed to be given a tune-up.

Our trucks were larger than the average vehicle, and our drivers, many times would catch the edge or corner, of a garage, shop, car-port, house, tree, or limbs. These little boo, boos, are costly.

One of my pet peas, was our workers taking a coffee break,

for an hour or two. Not just ten, or fifteen minutes. Coffee stains any where they set their cup down. Smoking, putting their cigarette down and burning a stain where ever that thing was placed. Burning holes in our seats, chairs, vehicles, and their clothes, and the butts on the ground, or all around. That is what I observed, and learned not to do. So, to this day I do not smoke, do not drink coffee, ever, and have never tried, or wanted to try to drink beer, or strong drink. Why, do people do that? It's expensive to buy, dangerous to your own health, and others around you. Can get you killed, and kill others, due to stupidity, not counting the court cost, etc. I've made a lot of mistakes, like many others, but most of those are honest, and ones I try to learn from.

In and around Algoa, the Adair boys were up and down the roads, and highways, driving our tractors to all sorts of small jobs. Mowing a pasture for Mr. Johnny Flora, over in Floraville. (This name was given where ever the family names are grouped together). He lived across the railroad tracks in Brazoria County, about a mile from home. Perhaps putting in a garden for Mrs. Wilkes, a very precious widow lady we all loved. Plowing it first, then disking, (for her we even planted, hoed and cared for her garden). Mom or Dad would take her to and from church, the store, or where ever she needed to go.

Dad would clean the dairy barns out for the free fertilizer at all the Lilley family locations in Lilleyville. We took load after load of fresh, soft, stinking cow manure, from the milking stalls, feeding areas, and the piles of manure, to help keep their dairy clean, and healthy. We would stock pile the manure, and let it set there, and mature, at A&S, into dry, safe fertilizer for flower beds, gardens, or to mix some into a load of top soil for a yard, or whatever. Part of our four acres, was used for stock piles of top soil, fill sand, oyster shell, culverts for driveways in many different sizes.

Our neighbors and friends in and around Algoa had been talking for years, about starting up a volunteer fire department, (VFD), for the safety of our growing community. I mean, now, our population must be somewhere near the numbers of 250, if you count the cows, and the chickens. Some well meaning neighbors, had made some contacts, with other VFD's, and found there were old fire trucks that were free for the taking, and financial support from Uncle Sam, thru certain grants, and qualification factors. Algoa, VFD, held its first meeting, just to get a jest of how most folks felt about supporting one. It was overwhelming how everyone, just knew it was the right thing to do, and time to do it. The need for the right Fire Chief, was discussed, and would you believe, Mr. S.R. Adair, Sr. was elected on the spot. Could it have been that he had a work shop, and employees that could fix anything. He had two way radio's, a dispatcher, a wife that could drive the fire truck if a man was not available. The list could go on and on.

The Naval Air Station in Corpus Christi, TX, had two working fire trucks they had just replaced. The Algoa VFD. could come pick them up at any time in the next month or two. Dad borrowed a truck and flatbed trailer to carry one back on, and they would drive the other one. I got to tag along, and helped tie down the one they hauled back. It was a tanker truck, that just carried water to a fire, for other fire trucks to have water to use as needed. Mr. Pete Peltier, went with us, and drove the other fire truck back to Algoa. Now we had two fire trucks, and soon had a third truck. It was called a brush fire truck, and was an old Ford. Hoses, and much needed equipment was soon on hand. Everyone in the community seemed to be putting hands on to get a building up, two large water tanks up on a heavy built tower to load the fire trucks quickly.

The Boy Scout troop 23, that Larry and I were a part of, became trained, right along with the men in the area. The feeling was, that if there should be a need for more help, or firemen, the seasoned Boy Scouts, could be called on to respond as needed, and we did. All our Dad's knew the potential their sons had to offer. Larry and I had been driving dump trucks for years, just not on the highways yet. We did not get our drivers license till age 15, or 16 best I can remember. Mom could drive the fire truck, and did a few times. Dad had red lights put on his car, and all of our pick-up trucks.

It was about a year, or so later, that one night we heard an explosion, about 8 or 9 pm. We had just finished eating, and went to the back porch. The sound we heard seemed to come from the South, back of our house. We could see a bright flare like flame shooting into the air, several miles from us. Dad wanted to check on it, to see if the Algoa VFD could help. I went with him, and as we drove East toward Galveston we became aware that it was farther away than we thought. We got to Alta Loma, before we saw it was now due South. We went over the Santa Fe railroad, and drove South. He turned his red flashing lights on as we found our way down county roads to the fire. We came to a Galveston County Deputy, with his emergency lights flashing, and blocking the road. Dad simply told the officer he was the Fire Chief from Algoa, and his name was Adair. The officer told my Dad to follow him. So we did, right up to the oil well fire. It was the O' Daniel number two that had caught fire, and the officer thought he had Mr. Red Adair on the scene. My Dad did say I'm sorry, sure did not try to miss lead you. All I can offer is to help cool down some of the metal nearby, with our VFD. That was another memorable experience, with my Dad.

Adair, The Fire Fighter

Many times I've been asked if I'm related to Red Adair. No, not at all, but when asked if I'm related to the fire fighter, I pause, and say something like, that's my Dad, just to jerk their chain, before I tell them the truth.

My sister Lola, is five years younger than me. When she was about age 12, I taught her to operate the International 450 diesel, front-end loader. Yes, you remember, the one with the new teeth on the bucket. Well now the teeth are worn down a bit, but still have a lot of bite in the loading of materials into a dump truck. I helped her know when to lower and raise the lift for the bucket to work smoothly, picking up a bucket full, or emptying it. It is all in the timing of the tractor to operate it without spinning or, sliding the tires, and to not hit, or run into the truck your loading. It is a smooth operation, and when done properly, looks like poetry in motion. Lola got to where she could load a dump truck faster than Dad could. Now, that was an accomplishment.

Lola Joyce Adair, is named after two of Mom's best friends. Lola May Day, was a totally blind lady, married a postman, and had a normal son that has great vision. They lived in Alvin. She was really a great person to know. The name Joyce, came from another remarkable lady. Joyce Rymal, from Algoa, the daughter of Pop and Grandma Rymal. Joyce suffered from polio, when she was young, and was all crippled up the rest of her life. She was faithful to be in church, to sing, and laugh, just really good to know. I only told Mom, and perhaps a chosen few, that when I grew up I wanted to marry her, because she was so giving, and loving. Well the Lord knows best, and she fell in love with a Mr. Tommy Van Dyke. He too, must have come to love her deeply. They got married, and had several beautiful daughters.

One of Lola's best friends in school was Becky Mendenhall, Becky later married my brother Larry. They had a son Lance, and a daughter Rhonda, and lived in Alvin. You will learn more about Larry, and Becky later on. Lola, and Larry both had some near-death (A.N.D.E.) experiences.

(See A.N.D.E. Volume 2 for details.)

Adair & Sons, (A&S), dump truck and tractor work was still growing with our name becoming more of a everyday item in at least three counties. Houston, in Harris County for one. We were in the Houston area all the time. Getting new tires, mud flaps, all types of lights for the trucks, including emergency lights, and the list goes on, from STASCO, located on the North side of downtown Houston at I-10. We went to many different places for many things. Houston had a population of about 300,000 when I was about age 14. Riding into town with Dad, I saw them pouring concrete for the 610 Loop, the Memorial Drive along the Buffalo Bayou, and I remember a high pile of dirt, way out in the middle of a cow pasture. He said it was the location for the first Super Dome to be built in the world. That pile of dirt was there for about five years, as I recall. Yes, indeed, later on that was where they built the Astrodome, where the Houston Oilers played football. Inside the first ever completely covered, air-conditioned building of its kind. I do not recall A&S, having any part in the construction of that facility.

Now the building of the NASA, at Webster was a whole story

in itself. A&S (Adair & Sons) did help with that project. Of course, we were just a small contractor, and we were hired to help, by the larger contractors, like Brown and Root of Houston. They were the largest construction company in the world. We hauled in fill sand, top soil, and did a lot of tractor work, for NASA. We worked on this project many different times, over several years, as it was being developed. It was in both Harris, and Galveston Counties. As that area grew, it expanded into Chambers County as well. A&S, had the pleasure of re-landscaping the Galveston County Court House, downtown Galveston. We also had work in the chemical plants at Texas City. This included Monsanto, and Union Carbide. We (A&S), did work in others in Pasadena, Deer Park, La Port, and Baytown. We did get around. A lot of this was before Larry, or I could drive legally. Mom, or Dad would get us to a job, and we would go to work, doing whatever needed to be done. Now, we have worked also in Brazoria County. That is where Alvin, Liverpool, Angleton, and Manvel are. Another is Fort Bend County, where Richmond and Rosenberg are located. A&S, has worked in all of these counties, before I was age 15.

Some more pieces of equipment we got were two back-hoe type tractors, with a front-end loader. These we used to dig trenches, to lay water lines, sewer lines, and dig out tree stumps, and the list goes on.

The best advertisement we had was word of mouth. We loved to help people, get what they wanted. To get a garden in, have a driveway fixed, mow a field, plow and or disk an area, for whatever reasons. To dig post holes, was one of Larry and my favorite things to do. A&S, got $4.50 per hour for a operator, and tractor with three point hook-up. We would give them the option of just paying 25 cents, per hole, or $4.50 per hour. The customer would usually want to pay the 25 cents per hole, thinking how much work we are doing for only 25 cents. That is until they saw how fast we dug the hole and moved onto the next one. We would lay out where the holes were to be dug and come close to digging thirty holes an hour. Now at 25 cents per hole that's about $7.50 per hour. So, that is what was agreed to before the job was started, right? We still gave them the benefit of paying by the hour, to save them some money. Dad just always wanted A&S, to be fair, in all dealings, with all kinds of folks.

I always got a kick out of landscaping the yard, and leveling the dirt after dark. We would ask the customer what time they went to bed, because we could stop working anytime. Many times we could tell by their being hesitant, that they really felt we would be taking advantage of them by asking to work at night. They did not have yard lights for us to work by. How could we see what we were trying to do. The next day, when they saw the smooth surface, and were so happy, they would ask how do you do that. Dad would say trade secret. Truth of the matter was, we had learned to used the head lights on the tractor to show us the shadows. When we made our rounds, and the shadows were gone, we knew it was time to stop. That works every time.

Our Mom and Dad were very special. We called Dad "Pops" because there were so many of us that looked up to him for guidance, strength, encouragement, and the list goes on. Pops never said I love you. What he would say is, "go on back to your rat killing". I was about age 20, when it hit me like cold wet wash rag to the face. All these years growing up, he never said I love you. That was not the way he was brought up. So, to say he loves you, what you did, or the fine job your doing, he would stop and say, go back to your rat killing. That was an eye opener for me.

Thanks, Pops!

As we grew up, we had no pets, no dog, or cat. We just worked, went to school, church, and fixed flats late into the night, or worked on a truck motor, rear-end, brakes or whatever was needing to be done. He came home one day, like always, only this time he had a white puppy with just a few black spots. He told us in front of Mom, that he had been feeding that critter for a while at work. It had just showed up at their work shop, and hung around. He thought it needed a home. That was our first dog, but not our last. The one disadvantage a dog had around our place was Hwy. 6. It was just a two lane road, but had a lot of traffic on it at the speed limit of 55 MPH. We called that dog "spot", and he was loved. He was killed on the highway several months later. Another dog showed up later on, and Pops let us keep it, till it got killed on the highway. Our first cat was named Boots, all four paws were white. We started a grave area for dogs, and cats, and buried them with the front-end loader, or back-hoe.

Another stray that came home one day was a girl, Mom had picked up in town. The young lady was toting a suit case down the side walk in town, walking toward the train depot, and bus station was just over the railroad. I do not remember her name, but I do remember Mom got pretty good at getting those walking down the street, running away from home, or bad situations. Mom would offer to give them a ride, then offer to pay for the phone call to just let their parents know they are safe. Next would come an offer to buy them a hamburger, at Fords Cafe, or Harris Drive Inn. Some would agree to come home with her, for a good bath, and home cooked meal. She promised to bring them back to catch the bus or train, the next day.

Some did come home, some stayed a day, or two, a few stayed

longer, some were willing to let Mom contact their parents, get permission to put them in school, or help however it seemed right. Over the years, more than twenty-five found themselves at the Adair's home. Boys too, were given help to take a break from running away. I remember Donald Smith was from Alvin, and his parents gave permission for him to live with us, and go to Santa Fe School. Donald Parks was another, but he only stayed a short time and his parents came a picked him up. I think he was from the Houston area. No one was allowed to smoke, or cuss, and they all would help to get things done.

AGE 14

When I was a Freshman in high school always carried my lunch in a brown paper bag. We had a lunch room off to the side of the cafeteria that had several coke machines for cold drinks. At lunch time, when we got out of classes, there would always be a line of students waiting their turn to buy a Dr. Pepper, or Coke. I'm in line, when we all heard a lot of yelling up ahead of us. The two Springer brothers were known to be bullies, and they were trying to cut in line for a coke. I noticed how they would get shoved back out of line, by others. They would just go back passed a few students, and try again. This was repeated over and over, till they cut in front of me. They were several years older, but I tried to hold my place, and get them away from me. They caused me to drop my lunch bag, as they shoved me out of line. I came back at them, but they teamed up on me and took me to the ground. Now we are fighting in the dirt, just off our concrete walkway. The older, and stronger one had my head and neck in a "head-lock", and shouting at me to say "I give up", and would repeat the demand. He was really hurting my head and neck, and

I could not shake them off.

Pops had taught me all my young life, given any situation, always consider your options. There is always a way out, and be smart, take the one that seems best, given your circumstances. That was my thinking, now Ronny you were about in the middle of that line. You saw what was happening in front of you, so now, all those behind you, are on your side. Most everyone else is too, because you are trying to stop them. With these witnesses, I will make them "give-up". I faked, passing out, in their grasp. Yes sir!, That did the trick, they backed off of me so fast, and everyone is yelling you killed him. Some students had gone to find some help, and came back with Mrs. Mark, our History teacher. She was already told what was happening. She picked me up like a rag doll in her arms, and carried me to the closest class room, and I began to come around, as she sat me in a chair. I told her I was ok, just a little shook up. Someone handed me a cold Dr. Pepper, and my lunch bag. Mrs. Mark told me to just relax, and drink up. I heard what was happening in the halls, Mr. Lions, our principal was scolding them, big time. He marched them both down the hall, to his office, paddled them each many times, and expelled them from class. They were not to come back to school for three days, and then, only if their parents were with them. Always think "options".

Dad was truly a work-a-hollic! He worked six days a week. Five days on the job as a truck driver, and heavy equipment operator for Phillips 66 in the Chocolate Bayou Fields all around Alvin, 8am to 5pm., Monday thru Friday. Got off at five, drove home, or to the work that Adair & Sons had to do. Worked that job for a few hours, then come home, eat a bite, and work in the shop at home till 10, 11, or 12, & call it a day. Do that five days a week, then work with A&S all day Sat. till...?? Sunday sleep in, go to church, eat with the family, and relax till time to go back to Sunday night church service. Once a month, or so take a drive to Bob's Bar-B-Q in Hitchcock, for some outstanding food, to bring back home. We would watch "VICTORY AT SEA" on our TV, after church. FYI, we had the first TV in Algoa 1949, (as far as I know, that is what we were told, as we had neighbors come over to see ours, and watch it).

Mom could drive her dump truck like a professional truck driver. She was one, that knew how to spread oyster shell in reverse, that's right, backwards, better than some going forward. She would know how thick the customer wanted the driveway. Set her spreader chains on the tail-gate, start backing as the dump bed is going up, pull the latch, and make her on driveway to back up on till the load is empty.

Skating on the Highway

Once in a great while we would all get in the car and go see our ken-folk in Tyler, TX. We had probably taken this trip about six or seven times, maybe more. We always went by way of Palestine, TX. Distance from Palestine to Tyler is about forty-six miles. Aunt Reba, and Uncle Willis lived another four plus miles, North West off of Hwy. 110, out of Tyler. When Pops would first say, "OK, let's go home, get in the car. "That meant, use the restroom, and be ready to ride. Distance from home in Algoa, to Palestine is about one hundred eighty-six miles, add another fifty miles to Aunt Reba's home. It is at least two hundred thirty-six miles one way. Pop's doesn't like to stop to smell the flowers. He just drives us there, and when we go home that is the next stop. Mom would have him stop at a gas station sometimes, going or coming back.

Ron liked to roller skate anywhere

On this trip, Ronny Adair was prepared, for that first "OK, let's go". All six of us would be in the car ready to go, but Pop's is talking to Uncle Willis, and Mom is talking to Aunt Reba, out of their windows of the car. They would always talk for a while. Usually, this "talk" would last about an hour. Lola would get out, and go use the restroom again. Larry was fit to be tied, and not a happy camper, and Roger would be all over the place inside the car. I just kept saying let's go, and say that about every fifteen to twenty minutes. I had already told Larry and Lola, that when Pop's said let's go, I had my roller skates tucked away in a brown bag in the back seat, and I was going toward Palestine. You both have to tell Mom and Pop's to pick me up. Don't let him go past me. Watch for me, I'll be on the side of the road watching for you every time a car comes up behind me.

I waited for them in Palestine. Skating about four miles to Hwy. 155, then South on Hwy 155 to Palestine, at least fifty miles total. Passing by folks sitting on their front porch, I'd wave, and wish them a good day. Pops actually thought my actions were "funny", he approved.

Age 15

My first drivers license, and I was now moving equipment to the A&S various job locations. Pops had taught safety, and drilled that into Larry and me, that we knew to be careful doing anything, anytime. Driving to a fire, with our red lights flashing, siren blaring and speeding to get there, not to exceed the speed limit more than five miles per hour. He told us, you are going to help solve a problem, someone has. Watch out that you don't create another problem, before you help solve problems others have. Pops was a good teacher, by example, and giving tips he had learned the hard way. We would not borrow tools, and if we were working with someone, and using their tools, to make certain they were put up cleaner than we found them. If we were to get into someone else's vehicle, to just move, or drive it, not to adjust the seat, mirror, or turn the radio on. Adapt to your surroundings, and help be a problem solver. When hauling anything that needs to be tied down, to be certain it is secured, with plenty of tie downs. Loads we carried on the highway, would sometime be too long, or to wide, or to high, or to heavy. These required a permit from the TX State Highway Department, at a cost of six dollars each. We would always try to be legal.

Age 16

Age 16, the Algoa Boy Scouts, and us Explorer Scouts decided to build a log bridge, to put in the Scout Show to be held at Arcadia's Rungie Park in just a few months. We all worked hard on that project, cutting trees on the banks of Rymal's creek, and another creek at the Ketchell's place. Both of these were favorite camping spots, about two miles apart. The logs were tied together using only rope with various knots. When it was time to move it to Arcadia, three miles down highway six, we did not think to get a permit. It was wider, and longer than the A&S tractor trailer. The Mittlested twins, helped as Larry was using one front-end loader, and I was on another one. We lifted that bridge up, and backed the trailer under it. We set it down, and hauled it to Arcadia, using one of A&S pick-ups, and had the red flashers on for safety. I drove slowly, about 35 MPH, with the Boy Scouts in the back of the pick-up. We were about half way there when a State Trooper pulled us over. He gave me a warning ticket, and helped me to understand the red emergency lights were to be used only going to a fire. Ok, I learned that one the hard way. Best of my memory, our bridge did win first place.

Another Young Adult

Job # 1 Adair and Sons

With more growing years ahead. Age 17 to 21 gave me more opportunities to step out of my comfort zone.

Mr. Tom Cherry, the director of our Galveston Bay Area Council for the Boy Scouts of America, told me I needed to step in and take over as the Boy Scout Master of our Troop # 23 in Algoa. I told him I wasn't 21 yet, and perhaps some other person would be better suited for that position. He explained the options with others, and that the parents wanted me. OK, at age 20 Ron became their Scout Master in 1963.

About a year before this is when I became the manager of a Hancock Gas Station in Alvin. The owners of the Algoa Skating Rink went through a divorce. They had the skating rink closed. I approached Mrs. Edith Webb about the possibility of my opening it back up. She agreed, and the manager I hired to run it was Mrs. Albee, the mother of my girl friend Sylvia. Many responsibilities and it was all a very rewarding experience.

Still an active member of the Algoa VFD, I remember rushing to a fire, pulled up, got out to help, and saw that my pick-up truck bed was on fire. Got a fireman to use his fire-hose on my truck. The exhaust tail pipe comes from the motor, and has a bend in it to go over the back axle and on to the back end of the vehicle. That tail pipe had broken off where it bends and goes over the axle. Where it broke, it was blowing all that hot exhaust up to, and against the wood floor of the truck. That was burning when I got to the fire, with another fire. Fight fire, with fire, I don't think that phrase is appropriate, in this situation. FYI, the same thing happened to me about ten years later, in California, and I had five gallons of gas in the back of that truck. (see A.N.D.E. in San Diego, Ca.)

The University of Houston was on my mind, but when I visited their campus, it just did not feel comfortable. Perhaps because of their Snake Pit. That was the name of a snack food place on campus. It was in a dug-out, but beautiful trees, and landscape around the place to relax or meet others. When I visited the Houston Baptist University, that place did feel comfortable. Enrolled, and took a few classes there.

I struggled with the idea of being a preacher. Our pastor at that time was Bro. Billy Jack McKee. I loved him so very much. He really helped me with this serious matter. He asked me to take him fishing sometime soon. We did go fishing but I don't remember getting a hook wet. I was fishing for answers. Should I be a preacher? That was my question to him, and he told me God needs preachers and calls them. I wanted to know for certain what path to take in life. Bro. Billy made me really feel the Lord would give me a peace so great that there would not be any doubt. He reassured me that God also calls folks to be doctors, lawyers, bankers, truck drivers, equipment operators, etc. He made it very clear that we should always follow our heart, and enjoy whatever it is we find to do.

The Lord used Bro. Billy Jack McKee to help me realize that every life matters. That my life had been "UNIQUE" and so different from the norm in a positive way. He explained to me that while every DAD is special my Dad was the exception. Pops had taught me early on HONESTY and INTREGRITY, and a great work ethic that most don't have the opportunity to really appreciate.

He said, "Here you are Ron, you have been driving, operating heavy equipment, hauling equipment, running crews on all types of construction jobs, and you know how to weld, do plumbing and do electrical work. You are manager of two businesses and still work with your family business. You are a Boy Scout leader, teach Sunday School and very active in the VFD. You bought your own new dump truck in high school. You say you're ready for Uncle Sam to draft you into the Army, if it comes to that. Yes, Ron, you could be a preacher. BUT remember this; God will give you such assurance and a peace through His Holy Spirit to be a preacher, or to know the direction you should take. The Lord has a place for all of us to work, live and do HIS WILL. You have been a leader and teacher all your life. I feel the rest of your life will be just as UNIQUE, if not more so, than you or I can imagine". THANK YOU LORD, and Pastor Billy Jack McKee.

Used 1955 Red GMC Dump Truck

About 1959 A&S bought a used 1955 red GMC truck, and chassis, (that is just the cab, frame, and wheels. Nothing on the frame, or back of the truck. Most all of our trucks were green, with yellow dump beds. Our school colors at Santa Fe ISD, were "green & gold". We bought a new eight yard dump bed, and had it painted yellow at Clem's Paint & Body Shop in Alvin. Put the new bed on that 1955 Red GMC. Larry and I would race to the truck barn to get that truck. It was just fun to drive. We put an air-horn on top of each front fender. That truck had a few problems. It would twist the axle, breaking it, when it got in a bind, like getting bogged down in soft ground. It would twist the drive shaft, and have to be replaced. The transmission would go out, have to fix it. The motor would throw a valve. The top of a valve would break off and get hammered into the top of a piston. The u-joints would wear out in a short time. The carrier bearings did not last long. I told Pops, after two years, we should drive that truck to town, and offer anyone to take title. Pay them $500.00 to take it, and we would be money ahead.

FYI...countless axles, carrier bearings, u-joints, pulled the transmission 8 or 10 times to over-haul it. Replaced the engine three, or more times. Somewhere I still have one of the pistons with a valve head imbedded in the top of it. Used it as a door stop, and paper weight. One reason we liked it was, when you set the spreader chains to spread gravel or oyster shell, the front wheels would come up off the ground as you drove, and the dump bed gets higher and higher. At times, It would go back, and sit on its rear. When that happened, another truck, or tractor was needed to pull the front wheels back down to the ground. Front wheels would be seven, or eight feet off the ground. Often, when we had no help, we would have to get in the dump bed with a shovel. Then shovel the material off the bed to get it to come back down. That was NOT fun.

About 1962 I'm driving my dump truck from a sand pit West of Alvin. Going East, on highway 6, toward Alvin, and home. The road is only two lane at this time. One lane each way, and I come upon a car dead stopped on the highway, wanting to turn left. Their left flasher is working, but I'm meeting traffic that is going so fast, I know they will not see the car is stopped, before they see the left flasher on. I called home on our 2-way radio, and told Mom to call the police and send an ambulance NOW.

FYI... While she did that I turned my truck around and saw the collision. I positioned my dump truck in the center of the road way, emergency lights flashing, to protect those injured, and hurting, till help could get there. No one killed, but all of them hurting. I don't remember how many folks were involved.

About 1963; (A. N. D. E. ???) My dump truck has a left rear wheel come off, and pass me on my left side, facing traffic, not good. It had duel rear tires, side by side, and only lost one. No traffic was coming, the tire went off the road in front of me. I could only watch it go thru the ditch, jumped the fence, and came to a rolling stop a good 300 yards into someone's pasture. No one hurt, that could have been a very bad situation. Just rolled it back, could not get it back on, so I raised the truck bed all the way up. When you raise a dump truck bed, the top, or, front goes up, while the back tail-gate end goes down, closer to the ground. Used a tow chain, to tie the tire to the back of the dump bed, and when I let the bed down, it lifts the tire up, so I can haul it back to the tire shop. Got the problem fixed.

FYI, another situation...still About 1963 MY BROTHER LARRY, this time, is driving our smallest dump truck. (Just, got to warn you about Larry, he was the black sheep of the family). He really was accident prone. He crosses the Missouri Pacific Railroad track, on Mustang Road, South of Algoa about 3 miles. The dump truck, is loaded with dirt. Now, this truck only had a three yard dump bed. It has duel rear tires, (two rear tires, on each side). Only this rail road crossing, went across Mustang Road at an angle, almost no elevation, (no hump or height) and level, (flat, smooth, not much of a bump, at all). He goes across this railroad track, but in pieces. The complete rear-end, comes out from under the truck. One set of tires and wheels go one way, with the axle still attached to the hub of that set of tires. The other side does the same thing, but goes the other way. With nothing to hold the frame of the truck up, the load of dirt is still in the dump bed, on the frame, slides on the road about 60 yards, past the tracks. Larry isn't hurt, not even sure how it happened, he said.

FYI...Typical for Larry, he was not just speeding, he had to have had that truck going as fast as it could go, for a while, before getting to those tracks. Pops bought that small truck from one of the chemical plants in Texas City. His bid was the highest, do not remember how much it cost. I do remember when we got it home. That was the first time for it to be out of that plant, and it was about ten or twelve years old. All those years it had never gone over 10 or 15 MPH.

Pops used our wench truck to lift the back of the truck, put it on a trailer, and move all the parts to our shop. About two weeks later, it was back on the road again.

Job # 2, Adair Hancock Gas

October 1962 (age 19), Manager, Hancock Gas service station, Alvin, Texas, and still working with Adair & Sons.

Larry and I drove to the Hancock gas station on State Hwy 6 in Alvin, TX. to fuel up before going home for the day. It was late in the day but before dark. We had started the gas pumps when a fellow I did not know came out of the office asking if we were the Adair boys. He said, "My manager quit, due to a divorce. You fellows know everyone in town. Would you give me a few names of some older couples or an older man who might be our manager here?" I told him we certainly did not know everyone, but everyone did know us. We picked four or five names from the phone book and told him about each one. I also, asked him if he would add my name to that list. However, he did have reservations, due to our family business, Adair & Sons Dump

Truck and Tractor Work. I asked him what time he would open up in the morning and assured him I would be here waiting for him to give a yes, ok or no. He explained the hours, responsibility, pay and that they paid for one helper. He told me if it were ok, that he would really like me to consider the job, as long as the helper was working, I could go help my family from time to time.

I talked to my mom, then talked with Pops as we walked from the truck barn down our driveway to the house. Pops said, "You really don't know what you are getting into, going to work for the public". I responded with, "Who have we been working for all these years?" He told me it would be a good training experience and good luck.

When I got to the station at 6:30 am, the regional supervisor was there, so I told him it was A-OK. He taught me what to do and how to do it. He left, I hired a helper and started as manager. I worked there about four or five months, when Mr. Ben Massey, told me about the large Gulf station being closed. The two managers had a partnership in that Gulf station. They both had paper routes, and were doing more than just delivering papers. Some husbands found out what was going on and it backfired on the Gulf partners.

Gulf Oil Corporation closed down the station and ran ads in the Alvin Sun for a new manager. Mr. Massey had a warehouse in a building in back of the Hancock station, on Hwy. 6 where Adair & Sons purchased Amalie Oil products from time to time. We were close friends and Mr. Massey, helped me appreciate that the Gulf folks were looking at the applications to determine who would best help restore the integrity of that Gulf Dealership. My name was added to the list, with six other men trying to get that job. When they called me for my interview, I asked Mr. Massey to go with me. They talked with us, and explained the buyout of their inventory, the rent to be paid by the following formula: 1) a percentage of each gallon of gas sold, 2) a percentage for the sign on top of the building that when lights were on, read "Go Gulf", and 3) a percentage to pay Gulf Oil Corporation for the inventory I agreed to buy. Understanding their position, I now explained mine. Mr. Massey gave me sound advice as we were going through the inventory and the expectations. Items to take or not take, and only agree to buy some of the inventory. Their item # 2) was a concern of mine. Why would I want to pay for the cost of a sign, if in fact I was also paying for the electricity to light it up? It was huge (and beautiful), with "GO" in tall, white letters. Under GO, were three very tall and large bright "green arrows" pointing down at an angle to the word "GULF". This sign was about fifteen feet tall and traffic traveling West on Hwy. 6 could see it a mile before they got to the Gulf Gas Station.

I agreed to the 3/4 cent per gallon for rent, and the 1 cent per gallon till the inventory that I agreed to buy, was paid for. What I did not agree to pay was the 3/4 cent per gallon for the rent on a sign that would cost me to turn on. I would just leave it turned off, if I had to pay rent on it and pay to light it up. They agreed to not charge me rent, as long as I would pay for the electricity to turn it on. Half of the inventory was not bought, but Gulf Oil Corporation and I were happy campers.

I believe my reputation, integrity, work ethics and my skills working with people, is what gave me the edge to be chosen over six other older men. Ron Adair was now the new Owner and Gulf Dealer at age twenty.

Job # 3, Adair Gulf Service Station

February 1963 (age 20) Owner Adair Gulf Service.

It was like a promotion to now own my first business! It was a great feeling and I excelled in that opportunity. I had many applicants wanting to help me. The Hancock station got a good replacement, I saw to that. My staff of helpers for the Gulf Station were top shelf. They got to know me and my expectations right away. Working for myself was a joy. From time to time, I'd go help my folks. I loved what they did and how they did it. I had a girlfriend, Sylvia. Her Dad had retired from the US Air Force as an auto mechanic. He asked if I might want to take in auto tune-ups, repairs, etc. We talked about it and I agreed and gave him the #3 bay for auto repairs. We both made good on that addition to the Adair Gulf Service.

I needed to build an office staff. Loretta Thompson was a friend and neighbor in Algoa. She was hired to be my cashier, and run the office. She was a great help to oversee the business operations, write checks for the pay-roll, etc. Unfortunately, we were coming up short on our inventory and recognized we had a snake in the wood pile. He worked on the evening shift, did a good job but just was not honest. We did not have surveillance cameras available back then. He was caught red handed and fired on the spot. He begged for a second chance. I tried to help him understand, he chose to lie and cheat. He would have to prove his loyalty to someone else. We had many unique situations on my watch.

One young man I agreed to hire was Jim X. His Mom came to me and said, "Jim, bless his heart, just doesn't know how to do anything for anyone, including himself." He had graduated from high school but didn't know how to mow a yard, work in a garden, you name it; he was a challenge. I took Jim under my wing. I had him stay right by my side. I told him, he was to be my shadow. To just watch, and ask questions about everything I did. He was a slow learner but had a great demeanor about him. His Mom told me he had no clue how to check oil or air pressure in a tire. So he was learning and there was a lot to learn. A few months later, I had him working alone with instructions to come to me for any question, or doubt, about anything.

Are you ready for this? Are you sitting down? One day Jim came to me from the gas pump island where he had the hood up on a brand new, full size Oldsmobile. He was telling me the owner told him to fill it up with the best gas and check the hood. Jim said, "Ron, I just wasn't sure when I checked the power steering fluid, if I should add transmission fluid or what?" So, with my arm around Jim's neck and small talk, I encouraged him, as we walked out to the car together. I noticed the driver was in coat and tie, using one of our five pay phones. When we got to the car, I looked under the hood for the cap to the power steering unit. "Yes, Jim, you were right to add the transmission oil, but Jim, you didn't put that quart of motor oil in the radiator, did you?" A quart of motor oil with the oil spout stuck in the top was turned upside down in the top of the radiator where you add water. OK, now we had a problem. Jim said the man told me to add our best oil if it was low. He had just gotten excited, lost his focus on what he was doing and accidently put the oil in the wrong place. I told Jim to go ahead and fill the power steering unit to the proper level. I took the oil can from the top of the radiator and added the oil to the motor. Then went to wait for Mr. Suit & Tie to get off the phone. He was so patient and understanding and simply said, "can you fix it?" I told him it would take about twenty minutes to drain and flush the radiator and would need to do the same thing several more times before adding antifreeze. He did work with us to fix the problem and became a regular customer.

Jim asked if he were fired. I assured him that he was now a valued employee, because I knew that he knew what to do, and how to handle a bad situation. We used several gallon cans of radiator flush. I had Jim pay for half of that and half of the cost of the anti-freeze. Now there were three happy campers again.

Just Another NO, NO!

Sundays we only sold gas and oil, and fixed flats. Only one person worked, but two on call if help were needed. A customer came in midmorning, while I was in church. He wanted us to add rear end fluid to his car which requires using the high lift. I did not allow that to be done under any circumstances. My attendant was young and had no experience dealing with a customer who was a trouble maker and a jerk. He talked my attendant into allowing him to open the bay door, drive his car onto the high lift, put it up in the air, add the fluid to his car, and pay only for the three pounds of fluid and left. The young worker knew I was not going to be a happy camper. He took a scolding with as much patience as I could muster up. That customer came back two days later. He was cussing and carrying on like he had been horse whipped. He was accusing us of not replacing his rear end plug. All the fluid drained out and burned up the rear end as he drove his car. There was no reasoning with this "yea-who". He was belligerent to all my employees. When he and I did meet; it was unbelievable how arrogant he was. He threatened to ruin my reputation unless I buy him a new rear end. For several weeks, he kept coming back and I considered placing a restraining order on him to keep him off our property. Eventually, I did call a friend, Mr. Hornback. Owner of Hornback's Junkyard and sold a lot of used car parts. He told me it would cost about $30.00 for a good used rear end for that car. I told Mr. Mad Customer that he knew he was the only one to blame but that I would pay half of that cost, to Mr. Hornback, and for him to not come on this property ever again. He got his car fixed. He married my girlfriend Sylvia when I refused to get married before leaving for active duty. This was a total shocker to me.

I did not realize Sylvia had even met this guy. Sylvia and I had dated for more than two years and yes, she wanted to get married. As time came for me to go on active duty, she even told me, she would tell folks that she was pregnant. I loved that young lady and thought we knew each other. She had been in a military family. Her dad, retired from the Air Force, had lived in several areas, had two daughters, a son, and a very supporting wife. Sylvia wanted back in the military way of life, I guess. Me, I knew nothing of the military. For me it was going to be altogether different. I had just joined the Seabees and knew I was headed to Viet Nam. I did not want anything keeping me from my "focus" in a combat situation. No, I had asked Sylvia to wait for me to get out of the two years of active duty, in Viet Nam. We broke off our engagement just two months before I was to leave in the last week in March, 1966. A few weeks went by and she wanted to talk. She said she would wait and that was good news to me. That lasted for only a few more weeks then she came up with the threat of being pregnant. I could not believe it, told her we both knew the truth and that we never had that kind of relationship.

Another Driver Cannot wait

The Pepsi Cola driver arrived one morning while I had gone to run some errands. Loretta told him I'd be back shortly. He told her they were running a special and he was sure Ron would love it. He unloaded his truck and had cases of Pepsi in huge stacks all around the service station when I got back. He drove back to their warehouse in Galveston, TX. I called the Pepsi office and made sure they understood me. They were to come get every Pepsi and pick up their Pepsi machine and never come back as long as I was the Gulf owner. They did.

Another Owner Out of Gas

The owner of a gas station runs out of gas! My new 1963, Super Sport 409 Chevrolet was my ride to and from work each day. The Adair Gulf service truck was kept inside the station at night. Six months after delivery of my new car I was going to work and ran slap dab out of gas. This is on highway 6, four miles from the Gulf station and one mile from home. We had gas storage tanks at home too, this was very embarrassing. I could not get gas in that car fast enough and get it off that highway. I got a ride, got gas, and that never happened again!

Another Lost Trailer

Still 1963 and I'm helping A&S on a job in Alvin. My dump truck is pulling our home-made, all steel heavy, single axle, tractor trailer, from Alvin. It's about five miles, to home. A clear day, about 3pm on State Highway Six, normal traffic. My dump truck was empty, and the tractor trailer also was empty. Going 55 to 60 MPH, when I looked into my West Coast mirrors to check the traffic in back of me. I was shocked to not see my trailer. My foot off the gas pedal, I knew it was there just a few seconds ago. On my right, I see it out my passenger window, going beside me, and PASSING me. My foot back on the gas pedal, my truck is staying right beside the trailer. The tongue of the trailer is over four feet in the air, and traveling at a speed over 50 MPH. It does begin to lose momentum, and slows down a tad. When it starts to slow down it begins to drift to the right slightly. My truck is staying right beside it. As it slows, I go slower, and it's starting to drift closer, and closer to the ditch.

Now, we are going about 35 MPH, and the trailer is center of the ditch, this is a good thing, we are out of the traffic. BUT, were still in, and following the ditch, and approaching..., yes, you guessed it, a driveway. It just happens to be Mr. Hornbacks, and he has just pulled up on it, to go somewhere. He is looking both ways to check traffic, before he pulls onto the highway. That is what you do, that's normal. What is NOT NORMAL, that he does see, is the situation. He makes a quick executive decision to back-up, and let my trailer have the right-of-way. Good, he is out of danger, and my trailer is slowing down, just like a plane coming in for a landing. It would have been a beautiful sight, if it had not been so dangerous. Like a plane landing, the front of the trailer comes down slowly, AND PLOWS, right into the opening of the concrete drain culvert under that driveway. It could not have been planned any better. As the trailer comes to a sudden stop, the back of the trailer comes up, and the spinning wheels scorch the grass, and dirt, before they stop spinning. Mr. Hornback's driveway looks the same, it is just a tad higher on the West side, where my trailer is buried under it. Mr. Hornback pulls back onto his driveway, and told me, I had his attention.

FYI...The trailer was buried more than half way into his gravel driveway. We talked it over. I explained that with the trailer being empty, it was bouncing up and down a lot, behind my truck. The connecting pin had a safety pin holding it in place. The vibration had the pin jumping up and down. The safety pin just wore out, and broke. With the safety pin gone, the connecting pin just worked free, and let the trailer come free of my truck. We had safety chains fastened from the trailer to the truck too, but, when it came free, those chains broke.

Pops and I had built his parking lot, and driveway about two years ago. He said, Ron just fix it back. Assured him, it will be fixed this afternoon. Had a shovel on my truck, and went to work digging my trailer out of his driveway. Backed my dump truck to the back-end of the trailer. Used my tow chain, to pull the trailer out slowly. Shoveled the trailer clear of dirt, concrete, and gravel. Hooked the trailer back up, put a spare connecting pin on, with another safety pin, and drove on home. Loaded the sections of concrete culvert needed, and loaded one of our front-end loaders on that same trailer to make the repairs. When I got back to his driveway, it took about two hours, to fix it back like new. Tractor on the trailer, and back home, I called it another good day.

Job # 4 Algoa Skating Rink

(age 21) February 1964 Co-Owner Algoa Skating Rink.
The Algoa Skating Rink was built by Elmer and Edith Webb about 1958. Mr. Webb and Edith divorced. They closed up the skating rink and many folks hated to see that happen. Later they let me open it back up for business. We split the expenses and the profits. It was open every night of the work week for several hours, twice on Saturday and for three hours on Sunday

afternoon. I hired my girlfriend Sylvia's mother as manager to run, open and close it. This was really a great joy to be a part of.

Another Veteran

Job # 5, Military

(age 21) The first week of March 1964

Uncle Sam sent me a free bus ticket to Houston. It was for a free medical exam and testing for the U.S. Army draft! You need to understand, all branches of the military did not appeal to me on career day at school. My decision was to wait and let the Army draft me. The letter in the mail with my free bus pass informed me to be in front of our home on Hwy 6. The bus driver had instructions to stop for me. So I met the bus and when I got on, there was a ruckus, and four guys shouting, "OK, Adair, they got you too!". Dwight McCarty and several others had already met this bus. They also had a free bus pass. We had gone to Santa Fe High School together. They got on board as the bus came out of Galveston going West on Hwy 6 thru their towns first. Alta Loma, Arcadia, then Algoa where I lived, which is thirty miles West of Galveston. Five more miles into Alvin, then North on Hwy 35 on to Houston.

We got to the Houston bus station and off of the Texas Bus Lines at the corner of Texas Ave. at La Branch St. (Years later I would be Assistant Mgr. to the Ben Milam Hotel in the block just across Texas Ave.) A US Army truck was there, and an Army Sergeant told us "all aboard"! When we got to our destination it was a large airplane hangar at Ellington Air Field, just South East of Houston.

All total there must have been over 1,000 of us there for the same reason. The Sergeant told us what to do, "listen up". From the get go, waiting for the bus, I had this thought; this day will be interesting. Yes, it was. On a loud speaker came these orders, "Anyone, that cannot read, work your way to your far-left side of this building". Dwight McCarty told us that he had enough of this Army stuff and was going left and get out of there. So, he did go left.

They organized all the rest of us into groups for processing our individual information. We were asked what level of education we had; what grade of school we had completed, high school graduate or year of college. They asked a lot of questions, then fed us, then came the personal physicals (all very complete)! As we were being processed, I saw Dwight off at a distance with some others in a much smaller group. I asked one of the Army guys, "What is it with that bunch"? He said, "Oh, we always have a few that claim they can't read. They will spend the night with us but you guys will catch your bus before 4 pm today". When all was said and done, we were told we had passed A-Okay and would be up for the draft in two to three weeks. But if we wanted to go ahead and join some other branch of the service, we could do that. We were told it could take two or three weeks before we got our "draft notice". They said it could be a few months and possible that we would never be drafted at all. So, back home via Texas Bus Lines.

I was the oldest, age 21 then. My brother, Larry, 1 1/2 yrs younger, one sister Lola, 5 years younger and Roger 9 years younger. Adair and Sons' was still a big part of my life, working with them every day, except on Sundays. Other responsibilities that kept me busy were; owner, Adair Gulf Service Station, Algoa skating rink, co-owner and manager, Boy Scout Master for Scout Troop 223 (was # 23), Secretary for the Algoa Volunteer Fire

Department, and an active member of First Baptist Church of Algoa.

Just a few days after my free bus ride, Mr. Churchwell pulled into my Gulf service station in Alvin. He saw me and said, "I hear that you are going into the Armed Forces". I said, "that's the way it looks right now, just not sure when. Could be sooner or later, I'm told". He said, "Well, the Seabees need guys like you". "Never heard of them," I said. He explained that they are a branch of the Navy, like the Marines are. He said they have a unit in Houston, on Old Spanish Trail. We talked a bit more and after he got his gas, he left. Then I left! Seabees here I come! Found them, it is about a 45-minute drive and I'm asking questions. Who are the SEABEES and why is it they are not well known?" Can I join up now? I just finished my physical for the Army draft a few days ago. My preference in the military would be to work in construction as I have 17 years experience.

The Seabees Officer of the Day (OD), listened to me, then explained to me, the Seabees stand for "construction battalion". This unit in Houston was MCB-22 (Mobile Construction Battalion). It was a reserve unit and the reservist meet at 7 pm on Thursday every week of the year. They do not take recruits in like me. He explained that I could transfer into their unit from any branch of the service. He suggested that if I really wanted to join them, that I go on down to Galveston and join the Navy Reserve there. Then get them to transfer me to MCB-22 at Houston. I was asking for his help to make that happen, a letter or note on a napkin. He said he could not write a letter or call Galveston but he would be in my corner and help from his end. Fine, I'm driving straight on to Galveston. When they asked if they could help me at the Navy Reserve Center I asked to talk with the OD. Shortly a Navy man said right this way, follow me. When entering the OD's office I asked if we might speak in private as I closed the door. I explained that I just left the Reserve Unit MCB-22 in Houston and would like to lay my cards on the table. I want to join here, transfer there and serve my country doing what I know how to do.

He made a call on the phone and said follow me. We walked back to the front where I came in and boy, everyone was rushing around and one typewriter was busy and the OD said raise your right hand, which I did. He said repeat after me. I quickly put my hand down and asked the nature of this oath I was about to make. He explained their position and mine, and yes, he would help me get my Navy transfer ASAP. I asked these four or more men, who had just set the flags in place and all their rushing around as ordered, to be my witness to this oath that I wanted to be transferred to MCB-22 in Houston, TX ASAP. They all agreed, I raised my hand and took that oath to serve in the Navy Reserve. I was now a member of that unit and to the ship USS Crow. To this day, I have no idea what kind of ship it was and never saw it, (thank you, Lord). All my life, I wanted no part in the Navy. This Galveston reserve unit met all day Saturday and Sunday one weekend each month. The OD explained that I should come in on Saturday, but on Sunday come in the afternoon, after church, when I had finished my noon meal. Drive time was about 45 minutes, one way from home. It took two months for my orders to get me transferred to MCB-22 at Houston. They scheduled me for Navy boot camp and I was in the Seabees now; thank you, Lord. Making their weekly meeting at 7 pm each Thursday night was a real pleasure as it became routine. There was a Chief Petty Officer Sonnen, in MCB-22 that lived in Alvin. We became good friends and began to carpool. He would meet me at my Gulf Station and he would drive us to our meeting one week and I would drive the next.

Seabee Logo

78 Ron Adair

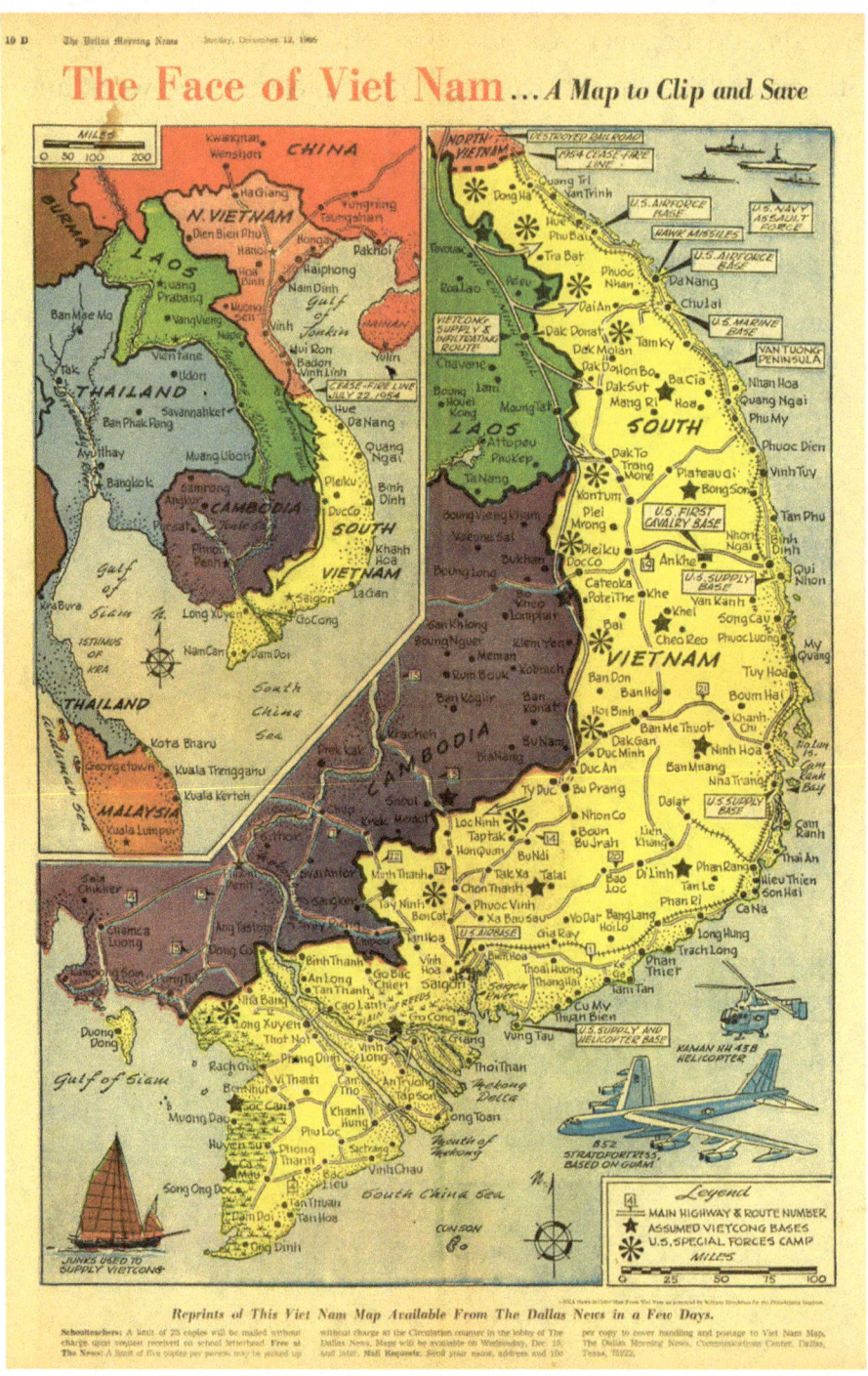

Map of Vietnam

Map of Vietnam

Seabee Logo ...Dong Ha, Vietnam our second tour

Seabee Logo

Seabee Logo

When I signed up for the Navy, the time of service was six years. Mine turned out to be two years on active reserve, (this meant attending meetings each month. MCB-22 met every Thursday 7pm to 9pm). This allowed me to be worry free from the draft. It also, allowed me to continue my work, and activities for the next two years at home. This active reserve time helped to teach me more about the military way of life. Following would be two years active duty, then two more years inactive reserve (no meetings). Navy boot camp was coming up sometime in 1964.

Larry's Texas Weekend

1964, December, my brother Larry is in the Air Force. He is stationed at England Air Force Base (AFB), in Alexandria, Louisiana. He is coming home for the holidays, driving his Harley Davidson motor- cycle on I-10. He calls me at Adair Gulf

Service Station, in Alvin, TX. He tells me to come in my service truck, and haul his bike home. It seems the freezing rain was constantly building up ice on his bike. The buildup of ice was causing the spark plug to jump fire to his leg. He could only hold his leg out so long, then let it rest, but the spark would jump to his leg again.

This would shock him several times till he moved his leg again, and again. He was waiting at Stuckey's, near Orange, TX. It took me over two hours to get there. He was still wet, and looked like a drowned rat. We got him into some dry clothes, and loaded his bike in the back of my pick-up, and went home.

We all enjoyed the holidays, and he drove back to his AFB in better weather. FYI, Larry is a Fireman in the Air Force, he can take the heat, but doesn't like the cold.

When "boot-camp" time came, the Navy had 1000 too many for both locations, San Diego, California, and the Great Lakes. They held a temporary third boot camp location in Corpus Christi, Texas, at the Naval Air Station there. My orders were to board a plane at Hobby Airport in Houston and take my first ever air plane ride, to Corpus Christi, Texas (approx. 250 miles South). Texas has always been dear to my heart.

Little did I know that the King Ranch reached all the way to the Gulf of Mexico. We marched on that ranch up and down the Gulf coast in deep sand with our right thumb inside our pants and fingers inside the belt and pants of the person in front of us. That was how they taught us to march in step, because if you're out of step you are being stomped on by the person in front as well as the person in back of you. We learned quick, how to stay in step!

This "boot camp" training was challenging in many ways, but

not over bearing. They were training us to follow orders, to be respectful, disciplined and faithful to each other. At one time I was caught talking when we were to be quiet. I was told to put my socks in my mouth - OK, I did that, probably for 10 minutes. It was good to take them out. I remember how embarrassed it made me feel, but better for it! We had some important duties, like "the clothes line watch". To make certain that no one snuck into our Naval Air Station, to steel our clothes line, we took turns during the night guarding it. When our boot camp was over, we graduated from E-1, to E-2. We had study requirements to complete, over a period of time. E-3 would be our next rank, and to reach that we had to be on active duty for a month or so.

The plane ride back to Houston after graduation from boot camp was just as scary as flying from Houston. To and from Corpus Christi, the DC-8 propeller plane would come into air pockets that caused the plane to literally fall then catch itself and your stomach and breath would gasp and pull at you! I did not like to fly till later on jet planes, that was A-OK, not bad at all.

A few weeks after boot camp, our unit MCB-22 was called on to fly to a city that had severe damage due to storms. Trees and utility poles were down, homes destroyed, etc. We did help clean up and set tall poles at the football field for the lights and power there. I remember it was out of state, I think Mississippi. That plane ride to and from was good.

The weekly meetings went on and the next year in July 1965, our Unit MCB-22 served two weeks active duty at Coronado Amphibious Base in California. Our mode of travel was optional for each of us. I had never been to California, so I decided to drive my 1960 Adair's Gulf Service Station pickup truck for seeing the sights and driving the 1500 plus miles, one way.

Al was a truck driver, and helped with mechanic work for Adair and Sons. He had a son in the Navy. His son was going to be on leave the same time that I would be in California. Dad and mom let him have two weeks paid vacation to go with me, help drive, etc. That was great. We set out for San Diego on a Friday afternoon, late, about 5:00 pm. Mom wanted us to sleep Friday night and leave early Saturday. Check in time was noon on Tuesday. We were fired- up ready, so we left at 5:00 pm on Friday. We only stopped for fuel, ate, etc and back on the road. We took turns driving and drove straight thru to San Diego, CA. We did stop along the way and helped a family that broke down in the desert. Later that first week they met us at a restaurant and bought our meal. I was driving as we came into San Diego twenty-four hours, after leaving home. We pulled up to the stop light in front of the ferry, to cross the bay. While waiting for the light to change, I noticed in my mirrors, smoke coming from in back of my truck. (A.N.D.E.) Another Near Death Experience. July 1965.

Al and I got out to check, and a man in the black car behind me was talking on his car phone. He was calling the fire department. Al and I opened the camper shell cover on back of my truck. The pickup bed was made of wood boards, and a fire had burned a hole in the wood floor. We had our luggage in the back but also had a spare five gallon can, full of gasoline. I jumped into the back, took the can of gas along the front then the side of the truck bed and handed it to Al. He set it on the sidewalk a safe distance from my burning pickup. Next, I handed Al our luggage and climbed out of my truck as a fire truck pulled up beside my truck. They put the fire out, and chopped the burn spot out. The exhaust pipe had broken off where it goes up and over the rear axle. All that exhaust heat hitting the bottom of the pickup floor, caused the floor to get so hot it caught on fire, (this same problem happened to me about ten years earlier, in a company truck going to help fight a fire). The time was now 5:30-6:00 pm on that Saturday evening. The firemen were helpful and encouraging, knowing our situation advised us to get it fixed Monday ASAP and to drive as little as we could. We did that and got repairs made Monday morning. Al rented a motel room for 2 weeks and met with his son.

When I checked in on Tuesday, there was a total shock to me as we learned of our training. We were going on a Navy ship for amphibious maneuvers. The large Navy Ship is taking us off shore about a mile. Then training us to go over the side of the ship, climbing down with full backpack, rifle and gear. Going down the rope ladder four to six at a time, getting into these smaller landing craft boats. Each one carried about 18 men. Once you are into your boat, that boat gets in a circle with six or eight other boats, like yours, and go in a circle for forty-five minutes to an hour, or longer, before they head for the "beach". The beach is what they call "Little Vietnam" a village made for these practice runs. Your landing craft boat comes to the beach, the front ramp comes down, now you can see the beach and you go running onto the beach while mortars and bombs explode all around you. You take the beach by going on through the Little Vietnam village with more and more explosions going on all around you.

Ok, then it's time to eat and do it all over again - practice makes you sick, not perfect!

End of training and free to drive back to Texas, Thank You, Lord. Met up with Al, and we made a safe trip home. Back to weekly reserve meetings again, and carpool with Chief Sonnin.

January 1966, a Navy recruiter had become a friend, that had many questions about guys in the area that were prospects for the Navy. We would talk about their family, their interest in school, and at home. He told me not to get my hopes up too high. He said the Seabees were looking for those guys that had construction experience. He said the Seabees had set up a review board in Houston. I was one of several that may be selected to go on active duty with a higher pay grade because of my construction experience. My time for active duty was the end of March 1966, when my two years reserve time was over.

While standing before these officers, in Houston, I answered questions about my construction experience, as a foreman on the job, heavy equipment operator, truck driver, dispatcher, fireman and working with my family business. Also, as owner of several businesses of my own. They asked me to step out and close the door behind me while they "talked behind my back"! About ten minutes later, I was asked to step back inside. They informed me, that when the time came, they were sending me on active duty as E-5, second class Petty Officer, and I would report to squad leader school in Davisville, Rhode Island.

About March 29, 1966, I left for active duty. That was a five-week training period. At the end we had a choice of two duty stations. One was Antarctica, COLD, or in Vietnam, HOT in more ways than one! For me, it had to be Vietnam because I don't do "cold". Ok, I get my orders to report to Port Hueneme ("Hunamee"), right? It is in California.

I have 30 days leave time, so I visit relatives in Sparrow's Point, MD (Mom's brother). I had never met them before. I took a train to Baltimore. It was a short visit, only a few hours and then I flew home. A few days at home and I take my youngest brother,

Roger with me and we drive to Florida and help one of my new service buddies, Dennis Rutledge, move his wife and dog to California. Roger and I enjoyed the sights, and time together. Returning from Florida, we did stop to leave Roger at Algoa and spent one day visiting, Dennis's family with my family. Then we are on our way to Port Hueneme, CA. As we drove across the desert, it was 130 degrees in the shade. I begged Dennis and his wife to drive my new 1966 Chevrolet Impala, 4 doors with air conditioning. They would not, but they did let their dog ride with me. We did stop several times, and that dog fell in love with my air-conditioned car!

The California State Troopers helped us find Pt. Hueneme on the map. Its west of LA near Oxnard, CA. We got there and loved it! The Seabee base was one of three in the world. The second base was where Dennis and I attended squad leader school in Davisville, Road Island, and the third is in Gulf Port, Mississippi. The Seabees are deployed all over the world as needed, and any one of these three Seabee base locations is their main source of supply.

Port Hueneme is approximately forty miles west of LA (toward San Francisco). The countryside is rich in various orchards, like fruits and vegetables. Some are oranges, strawberries, lemons, grapes, lettuce, spinach and tomatoes. It is all so breathtakingly beautiful. These are large truck farms, one after another. The fields are divided by beautiful rows of very tall trees, no fences. They have very elaborate irrigation systems and some have gigantic sprinkler systems made on large wheels, long pipelines for water and sprinkler heads that are huge, shooting water over the crops for great distances.

It is a couple of miles from base to Oxnard, CA which is a nice city, as I remember, (now about 50 years ago). I am longing to get back there and take in all the sights. I did have an apartment in Oxnard in addition to the sleeping quarters on base. It was all very comfortable and memorable. Having my car there was a real advantage and pleasure.

"We Want You", like the GI posters, was what I was thinking when assigned to take an embarkation course back at Coronado, California (near San Diego). That was one assignment I really tried to get out of for very good reasons. MCB-Five had to have an embarkation officer. That person had to be an E-5 or higher. He was responsible for loading and unloading our equipment onto ships that would be transported anywhere in the world. OK, "reason was", I do not like to be on any boat or ship that leaves the shore. To be seasick is an understatement. I stay seasick from the minute it starts out. Now the EP (embarkation person) is trained to do his job. When called on he stays with that ship, or ships, until it reaches its destination. There is the "gotcha! "Navy was not for me, because I would be going to sea. Well, they sent me anyway, to Coronado and it was great! There were about 25 of us taking this EC (embarkation course) training. These guys were from other CB battalions, Marine units and Army units. The Navy instructors were good and they wanted us to understand from the get-go just how important it was to do it right. The training was about four weeks long, Monday through Friday 9:00 am to 4:00 pm. Off work each day at 4:00, wow!

MCB-5 had a good size group of Texans. We had the Texas flag flying right there with the American flag "in country". I worked all my life and never got "off work" at 5 pm, much less 4pm! This was a real blessing to me. I had been able to drive my own car from MCB-5 at Port Hueneme to Coronado. We had living quarters there on the base. Great food and anything we needed was available. Our first week there passed by fast.

There was a new Navy Seal Team in training there. What they had to do, and go through, was remarkable. We could see them from our class room windows. When we were eating, and they came in as a group, that was a sight to see. They were usually soaking wet, and tired to the bone. I saw them later go through five days of what is known as HELL WEEK. No sleep for five days, and intensive training all day and night. During this hell week, they were often taken to the cafeteria to eat. I was told that a good meal is equivalent to three hours sleep. In a class of twenty to twenty five, just a few would finish, and graduate as SEALS. FYI, know what "SEAL" stands for? Sea, Air, Land. (Now you know).

Ron, E-5 heavy equipment operator

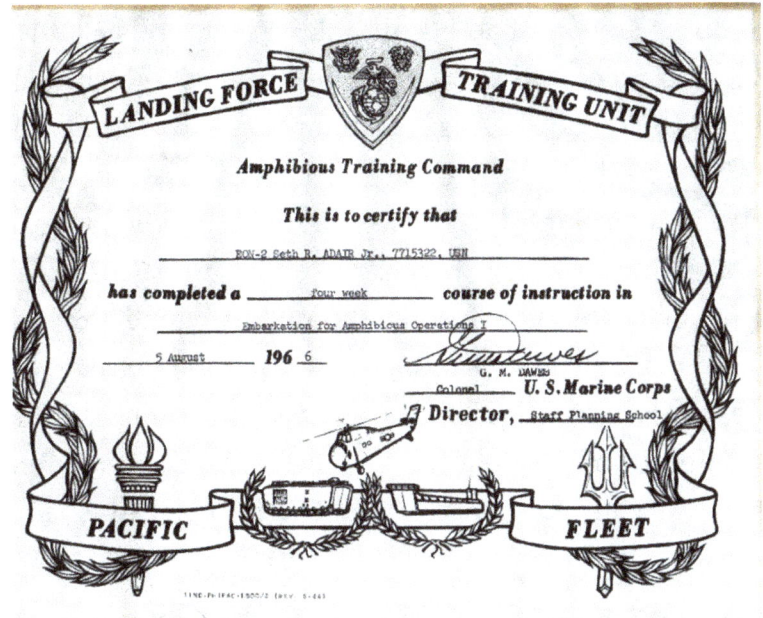

Ron servered as Embarkation Officer for MCB 5

We were given sheets of paper that had the drawings of each floor, or level, on a Navy ship that would carry all our supplies. Each level had compartments, or rooms a certain size. Each crane, wench, and the cable had load limits of how much weight they could handle safely. These cranes were positioned on the ship at certain points, to lift cargo into and out of these compartments. The first things placed in the lower compartments, would be the last things off the ship. Priority, was key here, so a dump truck would be one of the first things on, and last, off. An ambulance, or fire truck, would be the last on, and first off. Some of us stayed after class was over, just to finish our homework, and really review the days progress. It was rewarding in several ways. The instructors would stay around and help any that had questions, and this made it enjoyable.

At end of week one, we had liberty till 9 am Monday. Here I am, by myself in beautiful Southern California and a full week-end to do whatever. I had been thinking about this all week. At the end of class each day, I would try and make the best of this "free time". Coronado, CA is on a peninsula like Florida is. When I came here just last year with my Seabee reserve unit, MCB-22, I had driven all around this area, including San Diego. This area was somewhat familiar to me. So, during my first week of embarkation training, (ET) much thought had gone into "what to do when I'm free to go this first week-end". Going back to the Los Angeles area was intriguing to me. I had free time in California and wanted to make the best of it. Friday, when the class was over, my car was ready for my first trip into Los Angeles to see the sights.

The Adair's with two sons in the military

MCB-Five home base of operations, Port Hueneme

Driving on Interstate five freeway, out of San Diego, there were two guys hitchhiking. One had a navy uniform on, they both looked A-OK, not smoking, and clean cut. They got a free ride from me. They told me they were both in the Navy going thru training at the base in San Diego. They both lived in the LA area. One lived South, the other North of LA. Driving on for several hours together, you might say, we got to know each other. My bible was on the front seat with me, and that was one of the first topics for discussion. Passenger # 1 was a young man named Tommy Mitchell, & passenger #2 sat in the back seat. We talked about LA, churches, and where we each were from. It really was a great visit with these two young men. Passenger #2 was telling me where he would get out and catch a bus on home. He finally understood that was not happening on my watch. He gave me the directions where and when to turn to get him to his front door. He was so thankful to be home so fast. Catching rides can be time consuming and frustrating if you are a nonsmoker riding in a car full of smoke. Then getting still more rides to where you can catch buses, and finally get "home".

Tommy Mitchell told me his family was from Dallas, TX. They moved to the LA area (Receda suburb) a few years ago when his dad got a job building air planes there. Now up to his front steps, and he too, was home. The time was around 9 pm, and he insisted that he wanted me to meet his folks. "They are always concerned about my safety", he said. These folks made this ol' boy feel right at home. They fed both of us, and we all talked each other's ears off till whenever. They convinced me to stay the night. Their son, Theodor had married and moved to Northern CA so they had a spare bed in Tommy's room. It was a good night's sleep, great breakfast, (which seldom happens for me), and Tommy would show me their church, and we would spend the day looking around the area together. It was a great day, we enjoyed doing so much together. In the trunk of my car, were my roller-skates, so we skated some, saw a lot of the sights around LA, then stopped for assorted soft drinks to make our own home-made punch when we got back to his home. That was the best punch ever. His mother, dad, sister and brother all thought we were the best at making punch. Tommy and I had a ball. As the day ended, they invited me to go to church with them the next morning. Yes, great, I'll go on to the base at Port Hueneme tonight, and come back for church tomorrow.

Their church had a Baptist Pastor that was from Houston, TX. It was a great church service, and I assured them that this was the church for me.

Texas Flag w/ Texans; Ron is 2nd from L first row

Ron and one of his set of wheels in country

In 1966, for several months, I attended Christ Community Church in the Los Angeles, Ca. area before deploying to Viet Nam. Tommy Mitchell, a new friend, and his family were members there. I made many new friends there, and they kept in touch while I served in Viet Nam. They sent letters, packages of cookies, and all kinds of great things. This church, and my church back home were praying for the U. S Troops in combat situations. A lot of prayers were made on my behalf, and I felt our Lords watch care over us.

Tommy went with me that afternoon and we took in more sights. MCB-Five, Port Hueneme, and Oxnard were on our list of places to go see. Oxnard, CA. was for me a good city and near my base. When I first got there and reported in, found my living quarters, and got my assigned squad team with my orders to ET at Coronado, CA. I had not seen much of anything. So with Tommy helping me we had a blast looking around all these new places. We enjoyed the Seabee Museum, and the mess hall. The base there was big. There were a number of other MCB units assigned to this large base. MCB- 9 and 10 were just like 5, each unit had over 1000 guys in it, still more units were a part of this base, but they were serving in Vietnam, Wake, Guam, and all over the world. My unit, like 9 & 10 were serving in Vietnam. Tommy and I ended our sightseeing as we pulled into his own drive way. Just a short visit with his folks and we were off for San Diego. We made plans to meet that next week-end, and yes, it too was another adventure.

Now he was back getting his training, and same with me at ET on the amphibious base at Coronado. It was another good week (#2) for me, and really looking forward to meeting up with Tommy and spending time together again. We started planning what all would be interesting to go see, and do. We got to his home, and yes, spent the night again there. Boy, were we going to enjoy this time, seeing more of LA. We went to several different beaches, and saw a lot of the city itself. We drove up to see Beverly Hills, Hollywood, the "stars" in the sidewalk, Burbank, and so much more.

Construction of another boat ramp

On our way back to his home, we decided to make some more of our punch that was so great before. We're in the grocery store getting what we could think of that we had used before. We went crazy, thinking of this and that to make an even better punch. This time we added some ginger ale, bananas, watermelon, lemons, we really built some punch, but we needed a larger bowl. His dad's galvanized five-gallon water cooler would be the very thing. Right size, we could just refill our glasses so easy, and have still more than we did before. We were on a roll, adding all the various soft drinks, and fruit, added the ice and we were set. Well, it didn't taste just right, so we added more to it. We didn't have a clue on how to improve on it. So, we took on a consultant, to help make this the best yet, his Mom. We explained just what we had made in the water cooler. She came to the back porch where we were working on this project. We took the lid off, and she helped us realize our mistake. It was fermenting, right there, giving off this stench and small bubbles.

Building an AMMO storage area

Her advice, pour it out, start over, and don't add the watermelon, grapes, etc. We had a lot invested in this venture, and really did not want to lose it. Our consultant was right, when we poured it out, in the back corner of their yard we found it had eaten away the galvanized liner on the five-gallon water cooler, oooppsss!!! We gave up on making punch". (FYI, or Footnote, the next week-end to his home, we found out it killed the grass where we had poured it out). Not good! His family got a good laugh out of our adventures with the punch.

A muddy Situation

Finished my ET (passed) and found myself helping our unit prepare for our deployment to Vietnam. It turned out that MCB-5 was building a new group of Seabees, for that Battalion. This military stuff was all new to me. We were getting new men in everyday while I was in ET. Now, we were training them to operate the equipment we would use in Vietnam. This went on for a number of weeks. Some training was up in the mountains, miles from our base. We helped fight some fires, trying to save homes and lives. Santa Barbara and Ventura, were not too far from our base.

Time was getting near for our departure. An advance party was being formed with volunteers to go ahead and prepare the way for the group that would follow in a week or so. With the rank E-5, my choices of duty were; crew leader working on roads, dispatcher, or several supervising positions (like running the tire shop, where flats were fixed daily). These decisions were not easy. A fellow could get killed over there. The Lord is always with me, I knew that. At this, another cross road, He was very real and walking with me. My decision was to be dispatcher, and go with the advance party to Vietnam. As a squad leader, it was my responsibility to help the 12 guys assigned to me. We had been training together now for a while.

Future home for ammunition storage

Another True Texan Survivor   101

The advance party would leave shortly. Friends being left behind included Tommy, his family, and their church family, (where church times found me with them, when the doors were open). My sister Lola, with Mom, came out to see me off and drive my car back home. We enjoyed the time together, not knowing what the future would hold for me, or for them. Their visit was very special; we are a tight family.

They went their way, and the advance party left the shores of California flying in a C-130 cargo plane bound for Vietnam. Don't get ahead of me, our first stop was in Hawaii. There we ate, while the plane got fuel, then four hours later back into the air. Next stop, Wake Island, then Guam, then on to the Philippines. All were short stops, but very, very long hops, to get us to Vietnam. Our flying time, from Ca. to Viet Nam was three and a half days and nights. From the Philippine Islands, we were flown on in to the air field at Da Nang, Vietnam. We could see out the few windows of our plane, a first view of the country we would call home for some time.

As our plane was approaching the airfield, the plane came under attack by mortar fire, just as we were about to touch down on the run-way. Our pilots turned the plane to the left, put on more speed, and our tires on the left side just touched the run way, as we stayed air-born. We flew back to the Philippines. We ate, got the plane fueled up again, and waited for the pilots to get the all clear to try again.

This time the pilot told us in advance that he would land but not stop the plane. We got back to the Da Nang airport, and landed just before dark. He kept his word; he had the back ramp down as he slowed the plane to a crawl. We were throwing our gear, and supplies off, then driving our jeep off the plane, all so fast. There were men and trucks, waiting to get us safely to the assigned Seabee base. Welcome to Vietnam! This was day one "in country" as they called it. Our base of operations there was located on the sands of China Beach. Camp Adnier, was its name, almost "Adair", I thought. It was named after a Chief Petty Officer who was killed there. Now looking at our new home, we started getting things situated, and assigning what would be the layout for our troops when they arrived in a week or so. This was why I volunteered to come. To be able to locate the hut for my squad, getting behind the biggest sand dune, and out of the line of fire from any direction. These were good intentions. My thinking was stinking, as I found out in a few months, WHY. We were ready when MCB-5 landed at the Da Nang airport. We were operational from the start. (FYI, we have two "yearbooks" that are action packed, about the two tours MCB-5 was "in country". So I'm going to make this short...?

In Viet Nam "church" was meeting with our Chaplain, and he was a Baptist, also from Texas. At times our worship was interrupted with "incoming rockets, mortars and attacks on our base. I was scared at times, but I always had a peace that put the time and place in perspective. Many hours were spent, as I was encouraging others more fearful, that the Bible tells us not to fear 365 times. We built a Chapel on our base near China Beach, in Viet Nam.

Remember me volunteering to be dispatcher? That was so I could stay on the base where I would be "SAFE". Our base got hammered by mortars, and rockets, just about every day, often two or three times a day. Our jeeps, trucks, dump trucks, TM's=transit-mixers/ok, concrete trucks, road crews, builders hauling the materials to various projects, etc., gets dispatched out in the morning each day. The guys come back onto the base, check their equipment in at the end of the day. They ask, "ok, who's hut got blown away today?" They were right, we got hit at our shops, where our mechanics were working on equipment. Hit at the tire shop, mess hall, HQ, living areas, and all over the base. We would hear explosions, and run to a bunker for safety.

Construction work on our Chapel

The guys off base, were working on roads, bridges, and all kinds of projects. Our base of operations was between Marble Mountain, to our right as you leave our front gate facing the China Beach sea shore, and Monkey Mountain, to the left. Just between our base and Marble Mountain was a large sized, group of "tents", to make up a field hospital. It too, was located on the sandy shores of China Beach. Marble Mountain, as it was called, was not large at all. It was a few gigantic stones sticking out of the sand near the water's edge. It looked like petrified wood reaching 150 feet high, (FYI, that's as high as a fifteen-story building), and leaning away from the ocean, as I recall. It occupied and area of about a city block. Monkey Mountain was several miles to our left, and just outside the city of Da Nang. Now it was tall, huge, and dangerous due to all the monkeys. The Seabees built a very large radar tower at the top of it. Driving up to the top, you had to have your windows up to keep the monkeys out. I made several trips to the top with supplies. We were told of some service man that planned to catch a monkey, but it tore his throat out, killing him. Not sure if he was Army, or a Seabee.

The North Vietnamese Army (NVA) enemy, were everywhere hiding and would shoot or throw a hand-grenade. Other problems we had with them were land mines buried on the road ways, and they would dress like the Vietnamese. They were hard to find.

Going to the showers from our huts every day, we were walking on pallets to keep from walking in the hot sand. We wore flip-flops or not, carried a towel and a smile. This one day, I heard a lot of shouting, was not sure why, till I saw the cobra moving toward the showers. Some had already gotten their weapons firing at that monster but it hasn't been hit yet. More guys were getting into the act. The cobra reaches our concertina wire barrier before it is shot and killed. Just another situation, after that I always wore my combat boots to the showers. I wrote home asking Mom to send me bluebonnet seeds. She did and they were growing in front of our hut. There were some local people that we paid to do our laundry. We had a rock crusher set up at a river to make gravel for many uses. We built a very large ammo dump and fuel dump, actually these were storage areas, built away from everything, for safety. In Da Nang there was a Texas size supply area called Camp Tenshaw. Navy ships brought in all supplies for the various branches of the military and they were distributed from this Camp Tenshaw. Highway one and highway three were our main roads of travel. One Marine base was often in the news back home, Khe Sanh located near the DMZ. This is North of Da Nang about 100 miles. From time to time our Seabees would be sent to help restore what was torn up by the attacks there.

Someone's special touch

MCB-5 had another piece of equipment for me to pick up at Camp Tinshaw. It was a new dragline, with a two yard bucket.

FYI, two yards will fill up two pick-up trucks. This was a new Northwest 6, 35 Ton Crane, 60 ft. boom, 30 inch pads (tracks to move around on), Murphy 6 diesel engine, and it was just scrap. It had completely rusted down with corrosion on the underside, round table, and was totally useless. It made me sick, to see that fine machine go to waste due to neglect, and slipping through the cracks of military inventory. My best guess is that it had been delivered to Wake Island, or another like it, and had set there in the salt sea mist, doing the damage over a short period of time.

Pieces of shrapnel I pulled out of a utility pole

We were warned about swimming in the China Sea in front of our base. There were strong under-toes, that could carry a person out to sea, no matter how good a swimmer you were. You could hear the pay loads of bombs exploded in the distance from the B-52 Bombers. Night time you could also see the flashes of light as these bombs exploded. The roads were used by native folks, walking to and from their destinations. It was common to see them just step off to the side of the road, squat down and relieve themselves, when they had "to go". The city of Da Nang was to me, a dirty place. It was so busy, so many walking fast, bicycles, a person pulling someone sitting in a two wheeled cart, and so many old cars, buses, and trucks. All kinds of colors, but you saw a lot of green and white. The ladies wore white, with a round white hat, pointed up in the center.

I saw Bob Hope's show two different times when he paid the GI's a visit while I served two tours in country. When he came in, the security was so tight all around Da Nang. There was an open area on hill 327 where thousands of military folks could enjoy his show. It was so refreshing to see and hear his show. He had such great love for the GI, and he traveled all over the world with his show, and made us proud of the USA. I saw Martha Ray one time, going down the hall on an Army base near Da Nang. She was famous for her big mouth. Most of my time was spent on our base, as dispatcher. We got hit so many times, I requested that another Second-Class Petty Officer replacement take my place. Told our Chief Petty Officer to let me help in the field, and run a crew working on the roads. Before that came about, we had a new young man assigned to Alpha Company. We were told he is a truck driver. I cannot take credit, or the blame, but when he got squared away and reported to us for duty, I heard someone tell him to go on down to the tire shop. Tell them to give you an enter-tube for a fifth wheel, and bring it up here to us. We have someone coming to pick it up. The guys at the tire shop, told him to go over to the mechanics small shop to get it, and the guys there sent him to the big shop. They helped him understand, everyone was yanking his chain. A fifth wheel does not have an enter-tube. FYI, a fifth wheel is the heavy round plate mounted on back of a semi-truck, that holds the trailer in place, as the truck moves, and turns.

Our MCB-5 unit would get more pieces of heavy equipment from time to time. I took a truck and trailer to carry back a motor-grader from Camp Tinshaw. It did not look like any piece of equipment I had ever seen, when I first saw it. I climbed up on it to put it on the trailer, and the manufactures identification plate read: made by Westinghouse, / LeTourneau. The name Westinghouse was familiar to me, they made washing machines, and dryers. Who was LeTourneau? I did make some inquiries about that name. I Was informed that R.G. LeTourneau had invented the electric wheel, and made many types of earth moving equipment, in Longview, Texas. We did not have "google" to help us find out things in 1966-67. This motor grader could climb a wall to some extent, with its front wheel drive to help. I learned that Mr. R.G. LeTourneau wrote a book called "MOVER OF MEN AND MOUNTAINS". In 1946, he and his wife started a four year college in Longview. When I wrote to him from Viet Nam, he sent me a copy of his book. It was paper back, and very thick. About a year after I got out of the military, I attended LeTourneau College, it's a university now.

While in country, we were allowed a 7-day pass, it was called R & R. Rest and Relaxation, we all took it at different times. It was arranged before our deployment. Hawaii, was where I was headed, but some guys were married, and could meet their wives there. I gave someone my spot there. It just seemed like the right thing to do.

Atomie, Japan is where I was heading. Just to get out of Vietnam, most any place would be ok, and it was. I flew out of Da Nang, and landed in Tokyo Japan. Walking from the plane in Tokyo I heard good old American music on the loud speakers. Monday, Monday was playing, and I did start to relax a bit. From there they put me on a train to Yokohama, and from there a bus to Atomie.

My home for the next week was a modern hotel that was expecting me. The military was carefully looking out for those going on R & R. There was a clean looking young man that spoke good English, and helped me get registered. He told me the hotel had a bowling alley down stairs. He asked what I might like to see, and told me the cost for such a tour.

I did take a one day tour and saw a lot of the country. They had good American food, hamburgers, and steaks. This same young man went walking with me to look at wrist watches, at a jewelry shop just a couple of blocks from my hotel. The shop owner told me that Seiko watches were one of the finest. He explained that he knew I had never heard of that name. He was right, but he said you will. I came close to buying four of these Seiko's, but only bought one. It cost $25.00, and was self winding. I wanted to buy one for Pops, Larry, and Roger, too, but didn't. Enjoyed my short stay, but got back to the war zone. Our first tour in country was coming to an end. We had some in MCB-5 killed, and wounded. We came back to Port Hueneme, Ca. had a few weeks liberty before regrouping, and going back for our second tour. This time we were located near a village named Cam Lo, and Dong Ha up close to the DMZ, (FYI, Demilitarized Zone) dividing North and South Viet Nam. Dong Ha was just South of Quang Tri, and just inland from the South China Sea, not far from Khe Sanh.

A brass cross made from an artillery shell by a friend

This was an even more hostile area and we had to keep a keen eye on where we were, and where the closest bunker was at all times. There were more land mines hit. One blew up under a motor grader, causing serious injuries to the operator, and destroyed that piece of equipment. A rocket went through a dump truck door, and out the other door. That did serious injury to the driver. He was what we call a short-timer, due to go home in just a few days. Both of these men were very good friends of mine. They got to go home, but with injuries.

FYI, "agent orange" as it was called was sprayed from C-123 planes to kill vegetation that gave the enemy ground cover.

The "TET" in February / March, 1968, was to them, what Christmas is to us. The North Vietnamese Army (NVA), had been planning this TET OFFENSIVE, attack for some time. They hit our Seabee Base hard, every building had a lot of damage. It started early, I was on my way to the big shop about sun-up, when I dove into a trench for safety. Mortar rounds kept coming in, rockets whizzing past, and some artillery shells hitting our base, some were close by. This trench I was in, was just that, a trench. We had dug these with back-hoe's all over the place to give shelter if needed in a hurry. This trench and I became good friends, as I stayed there all day long. It was a long day, we had not had that kind of shelling, and certainly not continuous, as this was. I stayed hunkered down, but looking around as could, I saw a stupid guy running from one trench to another.

This trench had a wooden utility pole about three feet to one side. I watched as shrapnel hit that pole and stuck in it from every direction. Very late in this day, we were given the all clear signal. It was about thirty minutes before dark. I got out of that trench, and walked to that pole. I pulled as much of that shrapnel out as I could carry safely. It was sharp, and could still hurt someone. I put all that in one of my heavy work socks. I plan to get pictures made of it and add that to my ramblings here. Walking around to see just some of the damage, everywhere I looked, everything was shot up, and hit by incoming rounds. The next morning we started cleaning up. What we did clean up, had to be done by hand, because every vehicle, and piece of equipment had flat tires and other damage. I survived the TET, and two tours in Viet Nam.

Coming Home To TEXAS

Now it was the end of March, 1968, and my time to go home. When our two years active duty is over, we are replaced by someone else. They dropped me off where a helicopter would take me on to DaNang. Got into the "helo", and there were 5 body bags, going with us, (yes, 5 dead men). The White Elephant (military processing office), in Da Nang gave me the air plane pass, and took me to the Da Nang Airport to go on the big plane going to Long Beach, CA. non-stop. The plane to go home did not have any name or markings on it. When I asked, they told me it was a "Flying Tigers" plane. It was a big plane and only had a dozen or so on board. All of us were military, no others. They treated us first class, top notch, and made sure we were comfortable. I sat near the aisle, put on my safety belt, head phones for music, and the plane took off. Found some music that I'd never heard before. Paul Marriott, "Love Is Blue". That was GREAT! We landed eighteen hours later at Long Beach, CA. Made a visit to the Mitchell family, then HOME. Thank You Lord.

General Motors Acceptance Corporation, (GMAC).

Job # 6 Field Representative
(age 25) April, 1968 to August 1968.

One month after active duty in Vietnam for two tours. Mr. George Pearson, owner of Pearson Chevrolet, called me the first week after I got home. He wanted to help me with my career. He told me that GM finance, would be a great job and opportunity. Mr. Pearson was like another dad to me. I had known him all my life. A great Christian man and a real rock of a fellow. I went to Galveston and talked with the General Motors Acceptance Corporation, (GMAC) folks. They hired me. The pay was good, with a company car, expense account, full insurance coverage and worked with nice folks. Responsibilities included a running inventory of the GM cars and trucks on all the car dealerships in a five county area. It was a great job. What they did not tell me for the first two months, was that it had a dark side. They did not say anything about my responsibility for repossessing the vehicles that were so far behind with their payments. That was a real tear jerker for me. They gave me a list of wrecker operators that had no problem doing the job. When possible, it was asked of me to get the signature of the owner responsible for the vehicle on this form. We had the right to take it, no matter what, that's the law and these guys with the tow trucks, enjoyed doing their work. It bothered me that a few only wanted to do it the hard way. Sneak in, let the vehicle roll down the driveway to the street, or push it by hand away from where it was parked. We did not have to let the folks know anything. Just get the vehicle. The folks

I talked with knew the situation. Some begged for more time, or made promises, but all of it boiled down to just take it. There was a lot of this and it made for longer hours. Back at our office in Galveston, they told me to "just take the day off, from time to time. You don't punch a time clock. "We know what you're doing! It's ok."

The straw that broke the camel's back for me was Al Welling, at Welling Motors in Alvin. His GM dealership was right across the highway from the Gulf service station that I had a few years ago. We had met; he was all business and his sales folks were out to "sell". One of his salesmen had sold an old Rambler that they had taken in on trade. It was sold to a older couple in Alvin. The price was jacked up so high that they could not make the payments on their limited Social Security each month. After talking to the older couple, I told them no promises, but would see if anything could be done to help them. Mr. Welling might have known something that caused him to be so "cold shouldered" to me. He told me to just bring him the car. That was all he wanted. He got the car and I turned in my two week notice to move on with my life.

Just a short time after all this, mom told me about a wreck near Alvin that killed an older couple. It was the same couple that bought that old Rambler. They bought another used car, and both got killed in it. LeTourneau College here I come.

GMAC, the big corporation goal, did not work out for me. I quit, and I'm not a quitter, but I do know when it is best for me to move on with my life, (do you?). So off I go to Longview, to attend college.

Another College
LeTourneau Institute

College, and now University

August 1968; and two hundred fifty miles North of Algoa is Longview, where the LeTourneau College (University) is located. This college came to my attention while I was in Viet Nam. Mr. and Mrs. R.G. LeTourneau were founders of this college. This property was the Army's old, "Harmon General Hospital" on 156 acre site. It was deactivated on January 20, 1946. Mrs. LeTourneau commented later that it would make a great college campus. They bought it, and the rest is history. He was also the inventor for the electric wheel. He had invented many pieces of heavy earth moving equipment. One of these was the machine that moves the space shuttle to and from the launch pad for NASA. He was the largest supplier of bulldozers and carry-all scrapers for World War II.

LeTourneau University

In September of 1968 I became a Freshman and my roommate was Charles Deckert, a Senior that worked in the LeTourneau Mfg. Plant. We became best of friends as he told me more about Mr. LeTourneau and his life. I lived on campus in Tyler hall. They asked me to serve as hall monitor for first floor. Chuck, my roommate was from Wyoming, liked to play the banjo, and was a mechanical engineering major.

My classes were first year requirements; English, Math, etc. and Bible, this was a Christian College. The bible class was one of my favorites. Most of the students were guys studying to be engineers of all types. We only had a few young ladies that were students. Many of these students were planning on a missionary career. These were learning how to repair airplanes they would use to get around the isolated areas on the mission field. They had their own hanger at the Gregg County Airport. Mr. R.G. LeTourneau was a big supporter of Christian work.

Large machine at Longview, Texas manufacturing plant

Evangelist Billy Graham had asked Mr. LeTourneau to help design a portable building for meetings in faraway places. The five domed metal structures that are part of his plant in Longview, were the results of this request. The U.S. Army asked Mr. LeTourneau if a unit of trailers hooked behind each other, might be designed to turn so they could be pulled with each one turning when it came to the same place as the one in front of it. If possible to come to the corner of a block, make the turn, go to the next block and turn again, and so on. He did design it and built many unit trailers, all pulled with one truck. Where the truck turned the trailer turned, and so on with all those in tow. He asked the City of Longview to allow him to have a parade, and show this design in action. They said NO, because he would be crossing rail road tracks, and tie up traffic. I'm told he did just that, and it was quite a sight to see.

Only one operator and powered by electric wheels

His invention of the electric wheel is now used on all heavy earth moving equipment, all over the world, by all the major manufactures of heavy equipment. The Moon Land-Rover left on the moon was powered by his electric wheel invention. I could go on with more history, but my first year of college was great. Made many friends, and having my own car there helped me get some of my buddies to Valley View Baptist Church where they started a bible study class just of us college students. The Roberts family had adopted me from day one. Friends at home had told me to look them up, because they live right in back of the college. Mr. James Roberts was a butcher for Brookshire Bros. Grocery. His wife Thelma was a great cook. They had two daughters, Cathy and Caroline, both were straight A students in school. Cathy received a full scholarship from the Rice University in Houston, and became a medical doctor. The Roberts family were members of Valley View Baptist Church, and made my time in Longview, very pleasant. First year of college was over and I wanted a summer job that would pay well.

C&H Transport Company, Dallas

(Specialized Carrier; Permit Loads)

Job # 7 Truck Driver

(age 26) May 1969 I started driving a transport truck for C&H in Dallas, TX.

My brother Larry and our Uncle Tony both had their own trucks, and were "owner/operators" contracted with C&H. This company hired me for the summer to drive one of their company owned trucks. They told me they would keep me busy which was an understatement, and I drove off. This trucking company was one of the few that was referred to as a "specialized carrier." Their loads were mostly "permit", which meant it paid more, but, the truck loads were too long, or too wide, or too high, or too heavy, or too dangerous (like moving nitro, bombs or other explosives). I drove for them four months and had several situations develop. FYI, I was told "C&H", stood for "COLD & Hungry". Now it was time to go back to college.

Another Texan Gets Married

August 25, 1969 At Algoa, TX

I married Ruth Ann Burdett. A very lovely lady from California. You might ask, how did we meet? Her boyfriend, Tommy Mitchell was hitch hiking from San Diego, to Los Angeles when I picked him up. You read about him in "Another Veteran".

Ruth Ann and I just finished our Freshman year. She was attending Westmont Baptist College in Santa Barbara, California. I was going to LeTourneau College in Longview. She came to Texas to work for the summer. Before the end of summer, we decided to get married, and go on to college together. We were married at First Baptist Church of Algoa. Her father had divorced, and remarried and lived in the Los Angeles area. Her Mother and Dad both came to the wedding.

Ruth Ann's wedding ring was from Ed Nestra Jewlers in Alvin, TX. My ring was given to me by my best friend several years before. It was a gold and silver friendship ring, and now proud to use it as my wedding ring. We bought beautiful white China plates that had a pretty yellow rose in the center, and all the matching China dishes in stock. We went to Corpus Christi, for our honey moon. Ruth Ann was having her period at that time. She explained that it was normal, and not to be worried. What she did not understand, and it was very difficult for me to explain were the flash-backs of Viet Nam and all the blood I saw there. To this day, when I see anything red, it is turned to gray in my mind. We came back home to Algoa, and packed up for Nacogdoches, TX.

Ruth Ann's desire to be a Registered Nurse could be possible with the education at Steven F. Austin (SFA) University in Nacogdoches. This would be a move based on FAITH. We both felt it was the right thing to do, and the right place to go. When we arrived on the SFA campus, we were told that today is the last day to register and we had to have an address.

When we explained that we had just driven from South of Houston, they said we probably would not find a place to rent, or live, because the students already had everything rented. So we left to see what we could find with our Lord's help. First option we found was to be the married couple watching over a wood building full of young ladies going to SFA. A person could hear thru the wood walls, and squeaking wood floors. Not a good option for us. Next from the want ads, was a place on Old Lufkin Road South, and just West of Hwy. 59 outside the loop.

We came upon some of the smallest places to rent that I had ever seen, all in a row, on the side of the road. We had directions to drive past these small rent houses, to meet the owner at the house on the end. Yes, he was, and the place where he was at is the house that was for rent. Thank You Lord, yes we rented that one bed room, one bath, one kitchen and dining area. The price was fair, and it had a beautiful pond with green grass all around. He pointed to a home on the other side of the pond, and said that is where he lived. We could fish in the pond all we wanted.

We rushed back to SFA to register, Ruth Ann did get signed in, but we decided that I would find full time work to support us. She would help me continue my education when we could afford to.

Job # 8 Equipment Operator

September 1969 I found work operating a bull-dozer for Mr. Tim Christenson. His wife did all the book work for his construction business, because Tim could not read or write. He was a great guy to work for, had a beautiful family, and made fun out of work. I spent many hours reading my bible under the trees and around the pond in our back yard.

Fredonia Hill Baptist Church in Nacogdoches was our next church, with my new wife.

Ruth Ann had an opportunity to work and continue her education at the Methodist Hospital in the Medical Center of Houston, while I worked with Adair & Sons. We bought a 12 foot by 60 foot mobile home in Lufkin with the agreement they would deliver it to Algoa. It was set up in one of the trailer parks A&S built. It was owned by Mr. Joe Stone, who also owned Bay Concrete Products in Alta Loma. Ruth Ann was working at the Methodist Hospital, and I was back working with A&S. We felt we needed to be closer to her work place due about an hour drive each way. We moved the mobile home to 6127 Stuebner Airline space number "lucky thirteen". That's what I painted on our mail box at McCullar Parkway. We were one of the first to move into this new park area, just ten miles North of downtown Houston. An older couple, Mr. and Mrs. James Bond, a retired preacher had just moved their mobile home in first. They became great friends and neighbors.

Job # 9 Sales Representative

(age 27) 1970, Acme Fast Freight, as a sales representative.

Benefits were great, new company car and expense account, with good hours 8 to 5. We visited several churches, and finally joined the large First Baptist Church of Houston, downtown. We were members there for four plus years.

I had a friend help me build an eight by sixteen portable building next to our home. This gave us room for storage, and a deep freeze. Ruth Ann was a good cook and I liked to grill hamburgers outside. We would go see my folks from time to time. This often created problems with my Grandma, I think she just felt like being needed. She hid Ruth Ann's wedding rings one time, when they were put on the window sill in the kitchen. Ruth was washing dishes after we all ate, then she could not find her rings. She knew where they had been put, but were not there, or anywhere to be found. When we left to go home, my Mom said they will show up, not to worry. Several days later Grandma "found" them under something. That was not the first, or the last time that happened.

Roger borrowed a suit from me, for a friend's wedding. He put it on the hanger after he used it, and had it laying on his bed, for me to pick up later that day. Grandma was washing clothes, and took it too. It was washed with other things, then put in the dryer. It was now the right size for a six or seven year old. You really had to watch out for Grandma.

Ruth Ann and I took my company car on vacation to visit her Grandmother in New Jersey one year. They were good folks, and while we were there I built them an beautiful flower garden near the front steps I repaired. We had a good trip, but that company car used a lot of gas. I do remember that was one drawback to that trip. Six months after we got home, the company I was working for was bought out by Baldwin Enterprises in Dallas / Fort Worth. Everyone was laid off, about seventy-five of us were looking for work. Some of these folks had been working there for twenty or more years. My Mom told me that Myra Woodard wanted to talk to me about a job. I knew she sold insurance, and her husband did work with my Dad. This was about 1971, and I agreed to talk with her. I had no intentions of selling life insurance. She and her associates helped me to understand the purpose for life insurance. They told me you will either love it, or hate it. They told me what to do, how to do it right, and to always help others, never be rude.

Job # 10 Insurance Sales

That insurance company was Western and Southern Life.

I loved that job, and in less than a year, they wanted to promote me. To be a supervisor over six or seven other agents that had been working longer than I had, I wanted more experience and training. Ruth Ann I think, was pleased that I liked the work and had received several sales awards.

Ruth Ann's Mom wanted to move to Houston to be closer to us. Ruth Ann and I both wanted that too. Her mother was a very special lady, and a "Mother-IN-Law" that I loved. We did drive to California and moved her back to Houston. She visited several churches with her new work associates at Vincent Elkins Law Firm, down town Houston. She did join the South Main Baptist Church of Houston.

For more information on that trip, read about it in the A. N. D. E. chapter. What a vacation that turned out to be.

(See A.N.D.E. Volume 2 for details.)

About 1973 A&S had another situation when our dragline topples into our sand pit, and is under water, on county Rd. 99, West of Alvin. (FYI...) James, one of our heavy equipment operators, had been working for A&S (Adair and Sons), ten or more years. He was a good, very dependable, worker, but just failed to remember to back the dragline back away from pit where he had been loading dump trucks with fill sand.

For James, it was just another day, he just got off the machine, and went home. Next day we could see the top of the exhaust pipe sticking out of the water. The 50-foot boom, 3/4 yard bucket, cables, wench, turn-table, tracks, and cab was all under the water.

Because, of its weight; it had to be backed away from the pit area. It had to have at least ten feet, or more, of good solid ground under it, to support that machine. It took some doing to correct that problem. First, very expensive, to get it out. Then to repair the engine, it had to be over-hauled. Pop's had James, the E-O, do the over-haul, (he was the equipment operator, E-O, dig?) I think James got paid "half" his hourly wages on that project / or, problem.

Natalie Mitchell was a best friend to Ruth Ann, and the sister to my dear friend Tommy Mitchell. She came to Texas to spend some time with us, living in our spare bedroom. She did not feel comfortable going to the First Baptist Church of Houston, and visited other churches. The church she choose was on the North side of Houston, near our home. We went with her a few times, just to visit her church. Little did she know that the song leader had his eye on her until she was planning to go home to California. He came to our home and explained that he was told she was going home. He said I just could not let that happen without her knowing how I felt. She delayed that trip, and I think they got married. I remember Ruth Ann was happy for them. I think this was about the year 1973.

One of the patients that my wife was caring for, was a man hit on his motorcycle near Beaumont, TX. After he was in the hospital for a few months she told me about him. She felt I would be able to encourage him, and be a friend. He was a truck driver, so we had that in common. His name was Ron Harris, and lived in Buna, TX. I visited him often and we became best of friends over the two plus years he had to stay in the hospital in Houston. Ruth Ann became a registered nurse (RN).

I went to several parties that Ruth's friends from work had at an apartments swimming pool. These were embarrassing to me, and we left soon after we had arrived. Church was no longer of any interest to my wife, and she stopped going. We continued to have conflicting interest in each other.

Divorce

June 29, 1974. I was crushed, took this experience very hard. Yet, I was the one that in fact did file, and walked away from the love of my life. Many times, calls were made to our church, trying to get an appointment to talk with Dr. John Bisonyo, our Pastor. It felt like the church staff just pushed my request to the side. Never in the four plus years there did our pastor meet me or speak to us.

Ruth Ann got her own apartment, and kept on breathing. I took a leave of absence from selling insurance, and changed churches.

In 1974 I visited South Main Baptist Church the first week-end in July, and got there thirty minutes early. I had always appreciated the fact that SMBC had taken an active interest in helping Algoa Baptist Church when I was so young. Now here I was, going through a divorce, changing jobs, and churches. I was not a happy camper, and did not want to be divorced.

Sunday at 9am two "greeters" that met me were Mr. Al Kaiser, and Mr. Fred Sellers, both men worked with the folks my age that were single in SMBC. They were so supportive, and encouraging, as they understood what I was going through. On their Visitor Information Card, I did not check visitor, I signed up as a new member of that bible study group. Here was where I knew I belonged, and felt welcomed.

That morning, to celebrate July 4th, the preaching hour had the color guard bring the flags to the front of the worship service, while patriotic songs were song. Proud tears were flowing down my face, I could not hold back my emotions, nor did I want to. It was a previledge to serve in the armed forces, and I love our country so much. The song service was so touching, and the preaching by Pastor Dr. Kenneth Chafin moved me. I had planned to wait and go forward to join SMBC that night when there would be fewer folks there. When the invitation started, so did I. The Pastor met me, took my request to move my membership from First Baptist, and I felt so welcomed, and blessed . On their information card I filled in the blanks, and noticed the church sponsored a Boy Scout Troop, so I signed up to help them. I was given time and place where the Troop met.

Mr. Ralph Mills was the Scout Master of Troop 29, sponsored by SMBC. He and I went back to his office and I explained my situation, experience as an Eagle Scout and former Scout Master myself. We had a good visit and he invited me to meet the boys. He introduced me and told the fellows Mr. Ron Adair is your Assistant Scout Master as of tonight. Wow, I was not expecting that so fast, but it was a pleasure. There were two brothers in the scout troop that became very dear to me, as I met their dad, and family. Dave O, and Doug Smith, their Father was David M. Smith, Mother Charis, and their sister, Sarah Smith. Over the next few months, Mr. Smith took an interest in my skills as a leader, teacher, and talents. He became my best friend.

Ruth O., my former Mother-In-Law introduced me to a lot of friends at SMBC. She always liked me very much, and we could talk for hours.

Best Friend Dave Smith

Another, and another, but there IS NOT ANOTHER DAVID M. SMITH from Houston, Texas, he was one of a kind. He had his (EOW / RIP), home going Sunday, Nov. 19, 2017. This Dave Smith, was my best friend.

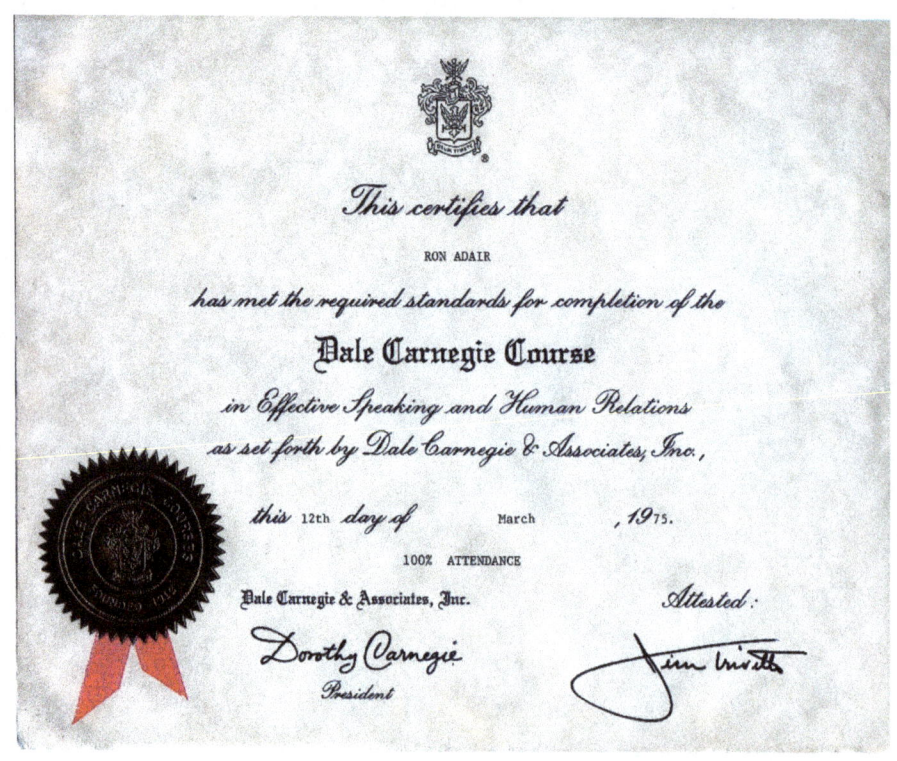

Training for Public Speaking and Public Relations

We met in July 1974, when I was working with Mr. Ralph Mills, the Boy Scout Master of Troop # 29. Ralph had a policy that the troop would go camping once a month, rain or shine, hot or cold. He kept a calendar in his office with the schedule of camp-outs plainly marked, so the boys, and most especially, for their parents to KNOW when those dates were. Ralph expected a

"DAD" to volunteer to go on a camp out with the boys. He told me that he, or I would always be on any one outing. Often we were both going, using his transportation, known as the "MILLSMOBILE".

Boy Scout Troop # 29

Mr. David M. Smith, was the "DAD" assisting me on a camp-out, that was on private property on the Brazos River at interstate 10, West of Houston. This "date and time" just so happened to be raining, and very windy. Mr. Smith, had two sons, Dave-O, and Doug, and a daughter Sarah. He asked me if we were really going camping in this rain. As Assistant Scout Master, I assured him that this was a part of the boys training in the Scouts. Yes, we loaded our gear in the rain at SMBC, and drove to I-10 and the Brazos River, raining all the way. We got there, unloaded the heavy canvas tents, and got them up, in the rain. When Mr. Smith heard me tell the boys we were going to get fire wood from near-by trees, he took me aside and said "Ron, do not paint yourself into a corner. You can't really expect to build a fire in this rain." I assured him "we will do just that, and be just fine". Yes, it was still raining, we were all soaked to the bone, and the wind was still blowing, but we had the two large tents up. I assigned one patrol to go find "squaw-wood", and another to get dead limbs of all sizes. A third patrol was assigned to get pine cones and pine needles.

All the boys admitted to Mr. Smith and I, that they had no idea what "squaw-wood" was. It's the dead limbs that hang in trees, or found on the ground. Just bring them to the location where we would build a camp fire in the rain. We did just that, as some of the pine cones and pine needles were put down first.

Then the tips of the "squaw-wood" were stacked around with larger twigs around that. Next, some finger size twigs, and then small limbs. Next we put on some limbs the size of your wrist. Now with several boys sheltering the rain and wind from this stack of wet fire wood, I struck a match. Holding the lighted match to the pine cone and needles they caught fire. It began to burn with the small twigs drying and burning ever so brightly. We had a great fire going now. Everyone was surprised, especially Mr. Smith. Now we are all inside one tent, changed into dry clothes and going to sing boy-scout songs to help cheer us all up.

The boys admitted they did not know any "boy-scout" songs. So Mr. Smith said, Ron you teach us a song, and we will sing it. "SOFTLY FALLS THE LIGHT OF DAY, AS OUR CAMP FIRE FADES AWAY...".

Now you need to understand, Mr. Smith was a better salesman than me. He took me aside again and told me we should take the boys to his home, and call their parents. The weather might make the boys sick. So, we put the fire out, left the tents up, and drove back to Mr. Smith's home. Sunday, after church we brought the tents back. Mr. Smith had gotten to know Ron Adair on that wet camp-out.

He called me in a few days and told me to just call him Dave. He had an old metal machine lathe in his old garage that he wanted "gone". He said Ron it cost him $400 plus moving, and if I could just make it go away, let him know how much that would cost. Perhaps someone would take it for the weight at a scrap yard. It was very old and heavy, it weighed about 2,000 pounds, or more. I took the Mfg. information that was on it, and went to a large company in Houston that sold machines like this one. A salesman told me it was so old that they would not be interested in buying it, but he said you can run an ad in the paper. He explained that Cameron Iron Works has a number of locations in and around Houston. They pay their workers for parts that they can machine at home, if they have the equipment to do so. He helped me write the ad and said, you will sell it the first day the ad is seen. Now the ad is in the paper, "FOR SALE $1500 Cash". The first twelve calls were taken, with their name and time they could come see it. They wanted to come to see it ASAP, so the first one agreed to come at 6am that next morning. The next one was at 6:30am and each one was thirty minutes later. Buyer # one came and wanted it, but asked if I would wait for him to go get the cash when the banks opened? I explained that the first person with cash in his blue jeans would be the proud owner of this machine. He saw my "waiting list" and said you will have it sold before I can get back here. My "6:30 buyer # two came and was very interested. He turned it on and started offering me half the price. I told him that the first person on this list that has $1000 CASH it will be sold. He pulled his money out, and he counted $1000 for the sale. He said it will be gone before lunch time.

Dave was very happy that it was "gone", when I handed him the $1000 and sales slip showing sold as is. He took $200, and told me to keep the rest for time served.

I noticed in the Houston Chronicle News Paper that Brown and Root was running a two-page ad. Just two HUGE words, "NOT" on one page, and "HIRING" on the second page. Now you need to understand, I was hurting with this "D I V O R C E" situation. You need to know I was mad, lonely, frustrated and just wanted to get on a bull- dozer and push something. I drove over to the Corporate Headquarters of Brown and Root in

Houston. Parked in their empty Visitor Parking lot, right in front of a big sign that read "NOT HIRING" in front of their offices. Walking up to their offices front door, a person might think it was a place to vote. The side walk had signs 12" X 24" on both sides with just two words..."NOT HIRING". There must have been at least six, or eight on each side of that side walk, from the parking lot to their front door. The receptionist asked me if I was here for an application? Politely informed her that I can read, but I would like to talk to their Personnel Director. A fellow stepped out from one of the many open doors down the hall in back of her. He introduced himself, and I asked if we might talk in private.

Back in his office I explained my reason for being so matter of fact with him. The truth was that Adair and Sons had worked with Brown and Root as a Sub-Contractor many times in the past twenty years. Now that I was going through this divorce, I just wanted to vent my frustrations. To push trees over, or moving rocks and the bigger, the better by operating a bull-dozer. You have jobs all over the world, and I know you have openings when an operator dies, quits, is transferred, or promoted. After answering his few questions, he assured me he would find an opening somewhere in the next few weeks.

I thanked him, and asked him to understand that my next stop was to ask AMSCO Transportation for a job driving one of their company trucks for a year, or so. To get on the road and travel over these United States, was my second choice. To see, and take in the beauty of America. The job opening that came first would find me available.

Job # 11 Truck Driver

AMSCO did not have any openings right then, but they asked me to go get my health card, just in case. Just a few days later AMSCO called asking how long before I could come to work? They had a driver quit, and his load was on the yard ready to leave for Oklahoma. I told them about thirty minutes, and started driving a big rig for them, till December of 1975.

While there I had several "Another Near Death Experiences", (A.N.D.E.) while driving "over the road" (OTR). Read about them in the chapter of A.N.D.E.

Driving a big rig based in Houston gave me opportunity to see America and get to come back home every week. I made most Boy Scout meetings, camp outs, and was in SMBC on Sundays.

Bells and Dave Smith

Job # 12 Consulting

1976 Dave Smith and I kept in touch. I had done my home work on the bell project. He had different guys try and melt scrap brass using a small furnace with a melting pot located on one of his properties. They used his patterns to make sand molds and poured the very hot melted brass into the molds. I asked for a week or two, to research the options, and he agreed.

Houston had several different foundry operations that I talked with. Mr. Keen at Keen foundry made castings for cast iron, but told me he would not be interested in making just a few castings from time to time. He needed to cast larger quantities for it to be profitable to his company.

Bells On the Move

Mr. Winston Woodard
Bell Pattern Maker

Mr. Skyvara was another foundry owner that made brass castings. (This is July 1974 and about 15 years later I will use Coastal Foundry to do all of our brass castings, to the present date of July 2020).It was much better to pay a tad more I told him, for professional castings that had the quality he wanted. He trusted me to get the castings, and contract out the work on the bells to have a first class bell. Driving the big rig had given me opportunity to do other things in my spare time, like the bell project. As I was able to get my mind off my being divorced, I was helping A&S from time to time. Later on friends asked for help with their insurance needs.

Growing through my divorce was not easy. One Christian counselor I was seeing each month had recommended the book "GROWING THROUGH DIVORCE" by Jim Smoke. That is a great book, and was very helpful. It helped me put such value on "relationships", "commitment", and the "attitude" we chose to have in trying situations. One very dear lady I loved was my now former "Mother-In-Law" Ms. Ruth O. Burdett. She was a very kindred spirit, so supportive and loving. December of 1975 seemed like the right time to get on with my life as I felt our Lord had better things for Ron Adair to do.

Job # 13 Insurance and Consulting

Life Insurance was still a rewarding career on my heart. I gave the truck keys back to AMSCO and became an agent for Great Southern Life Ins. in Houston. Dave Smith needed more Life Insurance on himself that I was proud to help with. That was when I became more aware of Dave's various businesses. He owned CXI, Chemical Exchange Industries, Inc. with three plants located at various properties on the Houston Ship Channel.

Dave had several offices across Houston. One of these was located in the World Trade Building on Texas Ave. Dave would sometimes eat at the Y W Cafeteria right across Texas Ave. It had a great reputation for its food and bakery, serving folks for over twenty-five years. One day, as Dave was taking his tray, greeting those serving the line, a lady with tears in her eyes, said "Mr. Smith, we are closing". I've been working here for over 25 years, and I'm too old to look for another job. That got Dave's attention and, yes, he bought the YW Cafeteria. All the employees kept their jobs and business was as usual.

The folks that sold Dave the Y W Cafeteria told him the Ben Milam Hotel is for sale too. Over time, Dave bought this whole block of downtown Houston.

Dave told me of another project that he had for me. He asked me to meet him there 10am on Tuesday the next week. The address was 1521 Texas Ave. at Crawford across from Union Station, (where the Minute Maid baseball park is now). On his side of the street, was the Ben Milam Hotel, Cafe on the corner, YW Cafeteria, etc., and the reason for our meeting. We walked down Texas Ave. to La Branch, then North, looking at his West wall and the "hedge row" that he wanted to just "go away". It was an eye sore, with a lot of broken glass bottles of wine, beer, and whisky. He said his employees could not keep it clean, because the Star Hope Mission was one block North.

Dave asked me if Adair & Sons could make it go away and how much would it cost? Yes Sir, my mother can come with her dump truck, and trailer, with a front-end loader. I can then take the tractor, and load this all on her truck, and she can go back to Algoa with everything in one trip for $250., OKAY, do it. We did, and he was a happy camper again.

He bought lunch at his YW Cafeteria, and said Ron the bell project will need your involvement from time to time to make 10, 20, or more bells. We talked about making another size bell. The 9 1/2" is what we had a pattern for . He wanted to make a larger pattern to have a 12 1/2", and I voted for a smaller 6 1/2" bell pattern. He said let's do both, so we did.

Long story short, I started working on the bell project in 1974, and that ended in 2016 when Dave was having health problems. With the help of Mr. Johnny Trevino Dave has bells he is proud of. Johnny was working for Dave in the Texmark Plant at Galena Park, TX. He started helping me at our bell shop, 105 Main St., (also in Galena Park), part time many years ago. Dave has given his bells to friends, associates, employees, customers of his parent company CXI, and he delivered one to George HW Bush, and First Lady Mrs. Barbara Bush. That bell is on the air craft carrier named after George HW Bush. Another bell was given to his President son George W. Bush for his ranch in Crawford, TX.

I enjoyed helping Dave with his various hobbies, projects, companies, and their challenges as it was beneficial to us both.

"Another time" Dave called me, was about helping him get three pecan trees planted in front of his home on Rice Blvd. This is a beautiful home across the street from the parking lot for the stadium on Rice University Campus. Dave and I looked at where he wanted to plant those three trees. At that time, little did I know that he had planted three hundred pecan trees at their home place in Dayton, TX. So, I encouraged him to go with one, or two trees, and allow for future growth.

No, he said I don't care if they grow their limbs into each other it will be just fine having a front lawn full of pecans each season. Ok, A&S did plant three, one Cherokee, one Pawnee, and one other, they did fill the front lawn. Just a foot note, years later as the pecans came, so did the Crows, and squirrels, and another call from Dave for me to help him with this problem. We put metal guards around the trees, put up dummy looking owls, and set traps to catch the squirrels. When captured, Dave took those with him to Galena Park and released them there, over fifteen miles away. Dave loves his pecans, bells, and people, they are so close to his heart.

Job # 14 Downtown Hotel

1976 Dave calls me again, with a problem at the downtown properties. Someone is stealing from the hotel, and the YW Cafeteria. Would I come on board as the Sales Manager, and Assistant Mgr. for the Ben Milam Hotel, and YW Cafeteria? It truly was a labor of love, as I came to know the manager of each, and their employees. The black lady in charge of "Housekeeping" was one of the most loving ladies I had ever met. She was so gracious about everything. She loved each of those under her charge. They were trusted, and she treated them so kindly. When there was any request for help in the hotel, she made sure it was taken care of 24/7. One of her problems was new sheets being stolen. Now this was before surveillance cameras were so available, and everywhere. Working with her, we caught the greedy folks responsible. Dave did not want to prosecute anyone, they were just fired, on the spot.

Ron, Larry, Mom, Lola, & Roger after Pop's funeral

Roger, Larry, Mom, Ron, and Lola

Ron's Mom and Dad

DEarest Ron, and HAPPY BIRTHDAY TO YOU...AND MANY MORE!!! Feb. 9, 2009

As I sit here in Lola and Jim's sun-room dining room table, I am lapping up sunshine coming through the glass windows, making it a nice place to recuperate from over a weeks's coughing spells I feel like I have finally whipped. Lola and Jim have also had the flu-like symptoms feeling bad, also. But they haven't slowed down one bit handing out a big bunch of TLC, which seems to be their specialty around here I am so blessed to be here with them. I thank God for them and the rest of my family every day, and that includes YOU!!!!

I don't know if your dad thought you might be born cross-eyed, 8 fingered or 12 toed, or just why, but he did not want you to have his name until after you were born that Saturday morning in our living room. But after you were born, so beautiful, white, all normal and with a smile on your little face, he came over to the bedside and asked me if I still wanted to name you after him. I said YES, and he actually shed tears. He was the oldest of 6 kiddoes, and had always had to share everything with them, UNTIL YOU WERE BORN!! You were his very own to have and to hold! To me, it was the only way to show my love for both of yall....We had expected to name you SETH RONALD, so we referred to you as "Ronny" so now you are stuck with that for a nickname

You were dedicated to GOD to be used for HIS Glory and after all these years watching you in your daily chores on the job there at McDonalds car wash and storage, treating customers in such a Christian attitude, I know that the LOrd has been your guide...your honesty and integrity are proof of that.To say that I am proud of you would not begin to tell you how honored to call you MY SON!!! Soon after your dad and I were married in 1940, I began to pray for a child, preferably a son, if it were God;s will....Three years and a day later, YOU ARRIVED!!

The doctor I had found just a few blocks from our apartment in Houston had formerly been the county doctor for Smith county where the ADAIR family was from. Dr. Grice had been credited with saving Tony's life earlier, so I was happy to have him available todeliver you at home with my own mother as his helper. WE lived upstairs in a duplex apartment with a nice couple across the hall way from our kitchen door. Valerie and Wesley had been over for coffee, so an hour later, when your daddy knocked on their door and asked them over to see HIS LITTLE BOY, they were amazed. HE WAS SOOO PROUD!! His dad never knew how to tell him he was proud of him, so your dad never knew how to let YOU know he was proud of you except by telling you to get on with your "rat-killing". meaning approval of whatever you were doing then....

You have been and will continue to be a Blessing to me, and to soooo many others whose lives you touch in so many ways. You are blessed with answers to other people's problems, especially Dave Smithand Marvin McDonald. Marvin doesn't seem to realize it, but Dave Smith does, so for that, I am grateful....

So, once again:::: HAPPY BIRTHDAY, AND MANY MORE..YOU ARE LOVED!!!!
I AM SO VERY THANKFUL FOR WHAT HAPPENED ON FEBRUARY NINTH, 8 a.m.1943

Your loving & grateful mother

I can't quit now...I haven't even begun to tell you how, through your school days you would drive a dump truck to school and after first period, you would leave, drive to Baytown for a load of mortar sand for delivery to one of the house forms I had filled with sand for the brick house to be built there. After delivery, you went back to school for the rest of your classes. All of your teachers knew the ADAIR & SONS TRUCKING included YOU and allowed special activities as such.. Also, after school each afternoon, you would get on our own C B radio to find out where, if any, you needed to load a

tractor and box blade to go level sand in a form I had filled..What

```
a BLESSING you were to us, as you were growing up  You never took any
wage or salary, so the 1948 GMC dump truck you drove to school was a
debt we paid for in 18 months instead of the 4 year loan against it.
You washed and waxed that truck each night before you went to bed....
You kept it ready for Lola to use on Saturdays to help me fill in yards
or more forms for you to level out later.  We were a TEAM..all of us
ADAIRS.  WHAT PRECIOUS MEMORIES I HAVE OF YOUR BIRTH, GROWING UP, HELPING
KEEP THE SKATING RINK OPEN BY HELPING EDITH MAE AND SON, "spider Webb...
     And now, at McDonald's car wash and self storage, you are once more
going far and beyond the call of duty, working lots of nights after 12
midnight washing bays filled with mud or grease or replacing broken
pipes or something else...just to keep the place ready for the next per-
son needing to clean up their vehicle.  You also work overtime on your
computor, keeping the numerical and alphabetical lists up to date on our
move-ins and move outs...MICE!!  You do all of this, yet youtake time
to help others with needs that only YOU cancome up with answers to their
problems or brain storm ideas they want help with...YOU DO JUST THAT!!!!
WHAT A BLESSING YOU ARE TO SOOOO MANY PEOPLE....HOW PROUD I AM OF YOU!!!
AM I BRAGGING???  NAH...I AM TELLING YOU HOW IT IS...REALLY!!!
```

Mom's letter to Ron on his birthday 2-9-2009

The sweet older lady that was manager of the YW Cafeteria also had problems with food being stolen. She and I worked on that problem as I got to know her helpers, and they came to know me. One day I noticed an employee almost to a back door, and he had a large box, that appeared to be quite heavy. I told him "let me help you with that door" and after he was outside, I said, "let's see what's inside". It was full of frozen steaks, which we took back to the cafeteria, and he was fired.

Another project to promote more business to his "block" was the use of passenger buses that looked like the old "trolley cars" from San Francisco. I made contact with the various courts in the court house where my brother, Roger worked as a court reporter for years. Roger also parked his car in the Ben Milam parking garage. The jurors that were sequester had to be kept together when the court fed them at various locations near the court house. They would call us in advance of time to eat, and we would pick them up, and take them to and from the YW Cafeteria. We ran a regular route in and around the downtown area. It was fun and profitable for all concerned. Prospects for the hotel were also developed providing sleeping space, lockers, showers, etc. for the crew from ships docking on the Houston Ship Channel, and the port of Houston. > Dave bought several buses that look like the street cars of San Francisco. They were used to run lunch routes around the Harris County Courthouse and several other blocks in the downtown area. We printed up brochures to promote the lunch routes and placed them in businesses on our routes. We got a call from the courthouse asking if it were possible to make special runs when the courts were feeding a sequestered jury. They had to keep those serving on jury together and separate from the public. Our 25 passenger buses were pressed into service when needed, taking these folks to the "Y W Cafeteria. This worked better than planned. Some people just rode for the pure fun of it all.

Jan. 1976, after making bells for over a year. I told Dave, the hotel basement had a large shop area not being used and would be a good place to work on the wood bases for the bell project. He was ok with that. The hotel had a health club area, where the ladies YWCA had been for years. It was on the third floor of the hotel. There was an indoor heated pool that was junior Olympic in size (BIG). We sold memberships to use the pool, basketball court and weight room. There were areas on the 2nd floor that were rented out for meetings, small conventions, etc. We could accommodate groups that wanted to rent areas with bunk beds. This worked well for the ships coming to the Port of Houston. We could house their seamen and feed them until they shipped out, then another ship's crew would come in. This worked great. One of the offices we rented out had a bookbinder business. We had a coffee shop on the corner of Texas and Crawford streets. We made some contacts in Mexico that frequently had groups coming to Houston. This and more made for an interesting life working for Mr. David M. Smith.

Brass 4" piece found when re-working Texas Ave. Ho.

The building had problems, roof-leaks, etc. Dave closed the property down with full intentions to remodel and renovate it all. The "new BALLPARK" was being built where the old train station was. This was just across the street on Crawford. One of the first things Dave did was to demolish one half of his block on the north side. This was done to make prime parking space for the ballpark. It meant taking down the old three story building that housed the laundry works for the hotel on the top two floors.

A parking garage was on the first floor and two floors below ground level. I was asked to oversee that project. The contract was given to demolish that part of the block without harm to the ten story hotel building. This went very well. All the metal, glass, and trash was removed first and hauled off. Then they used a very large track hoe, with a crushing jaw, to take a bite of the building and crush it to pieces. All of the "pieces" went into the parking garage to fill it up. Then another contractor filled in the area with good base material and black topped the new parking lot. Dave contracted the new parking space out for others to manage. This job was finished. Dave had an interest in a number of things. A few of these were bells, leather saddlebags, nutcrackers and donuts. From time to time he had me help with manufacturing, promotion and sales of each.

Job # 15 East TEXAS Bound

January 1977...Another call from Dave as he requested my riding with him to the East Texas area. It seems he has second cousins in Marshall, TX. that he has never met, and they might help him with another project. His kinfolks were Sam, and Bailey Mosley, both attorneys there. Their older brother Haywood was owner of Mosley Abstract Co. We had an interesting meeting of the minds, and Dave drove back home. I was left behind to mop up the details, and fly back home to Houston from the Gregg County Air Port the next day. This was in January 1977. This project was to find large tracks of land that had "LIGNITE" (low grade coal), under the ground. Dave wanted to get his three Petro-chemical companies weaned off of the chemical base they were dependent on. Dave already had contracts with the Eastman Kodak chemical plants. The one in Longview was considering a major change from natural gas to coal and lignite. Dave wanted to supply them their fuel.

With Haywood Mosley's help he introduced me to several local Realtors in the Longview and Marshall area. Mr. Bob Patterson in Marshall was the one realtor I had the most interest in. He, like several others, we talked about several properties and looked at a lot of "plats" and maps of the counties near the Texas Eastman plant in Gregg county. I did fly back the next day, and reported my findings to Dave. I was asked again for a period of time to "look into this some more" for him. This time I had packed a bag, and drove back to Longview.

Ron Adair's "horse" at Longview is a 4-wheel-drive Jeep to take him wherever he needs to go across the 4,967-acre CXI Ranch.

Now, another "foot-note" you should know is Dave did not like those who lied or cheated, smoked, or lawyers, (with the exception being his brother Paul, a best friend, an attorney with Smith, Smith, Hale, and Gunther in San Antonio, TX.) Did I mention funerals? Dave did not go to most funerals. When my dad died in Feb. of 1977, Dave was there in the second row.

Thank you, Bro. Dave Smith. The examples Dave gave from the heart, have guided me from day one of meeting him.

Mr. David M. Smith in Houston

Dave and those who led in each of his companies under the umbrella of CXI, were all in agreement of the soon to be 4,967 acre CXI Ranch in Longview, TX. I was the first employee of Dave's new company, Texas Lignite Corp. (TLC) and became

Mining Manager. A mining permit had to issued before any digging began. This permit would take more than a year to get approved. We had Mr. Jay P. Eggert, Vice President of TLC "getting ready", and that was a project in itself. The Surface Mining and Reclamation Division of the Railroad Commission of the State of Texas was our first major hurtle. To get their approval, the requirements were just under two inches thick. That was 1977, and in just a year the requirements for a mining permit increased to about four inches thick.

One problem we had was the beavers had built a dam across a creek, and flooding more than a thousand acres of our ranch. The right consultant was found that could take care of this problem. He had done work for the Texas Highway Department when roads would flood, due to the beavers building dams. This dam on our property had been built over a long period of time. It was over eight feet high, and more than three hundred feet long. That is more than the length of a football field. He used dynamite, and blew it up. Solved that problem.

We had a great neighbor just East of our property. Mr. Glenn Southerland, and family that leased several hundred acres from us. He reminded me of Pops, my father. He and his three sons were hard workers, and very talented in construction work. His daughter took welding in high school shop, and Mrs. Southerland was so supportive to their family in all matters. Their second to the oldest son was killed in a highway crash. He was about age 20. They had several dozers and tractors which they made all repairs on. Glenn designed, planned and worked with CXI, to install a huge drain pipe for one large ditch that drained into the Sabine River. Built, and installed it to keep the Sabine River from flooding our property in this one low area.

In 1977, toward the end of the year, I moved my church membership to Mobberly Ave. Baptist Church, Longview, with Dr. Laney Johnson, Pastor. The Minister of Music, was Mr. Dale Perkins. There are many fond memories while involved with various ministries at this great church. One memory, not so fond, was after I had been there a year or so. I received a phone call from our church office on a Saturday. They had a request from a fellow staying at the YMCA, wanting a ride Sunday morning to our church. Would I give him a ride, or should they call someone else? Yes, glad to help, they gave me his name so I went by that Saturday afternoon to meet "Mike". We talked for about thirty minutes, and he would be ready. He struck me as a person not to be trusted. I told our pastor about him that Sunday morning, and after a "short meeting" he agreed. Our Pastor said, "Ron, we need to treat him like a rattle-snake". Keep your eye on him, and don't get to close.

That was very sound advice, and we were in agreement. After church I took him to lunch, and listened to a lot of stuff that did not seem to fit together. He asked for my help finding a job, he wanted to stay in Longview, and join our church. His story was that he was from Houston, just divorced, and did not want anyone digging into his past. He would not give me any information on where he worked, family, or friends. That was just RED FLAGS, and I knew to be extra careful. He told me he was a "gourmet chef", and could prove so to any restaurant willing to help him get a fresh start. The places I contacted were told the truth, to be careful of him, because we know nothing about him. The Ramada Inn was less than a mile from the YMCA, and would give him a chance to prove himself. So, now he has a job cooking and I'm told he is doing great. He asked me to help get him a used bicycle, so he could get to and from work. We went to Sears, where I let him pick out a new bike, with the understanding this was my bike. It was only on loan to him. He was riding with me to and from church, while his bike was locked up with his new lock and chain to keep it secure. One day someone stole it he said. So now he is back walking to work.

During the next two months Mike and I had many meals together at our Luby's Cafeteria. I had a business meeting coming up in Colorado, and would be gone for a week.

My Car Is Stolen

December 1978

When I returned Friday evening, after being out of town, my car was gone. My apartment was not broken into, but my expensive IBM typewriter, camera, and large suite case were missing. I made a police report for all these things gone. The Mgr. of the YMCA, said Mike checked out Friday, and left in a cab.

Sunday morning at church a neighbor that lives in the apartment in front of mine, asked me if everything was alright. I told him about the things missing, including my car. He then told me that he heard a car door shut, so he looked out his window and saw my friend Mike. He said Mike got out of a cab, walked over to my car, opened the door, and put his coat inside. He then walked around to my apartment, and in just a few minutes returned, put a suitcase inside and drove off. Now, I know what happened, what I do not know is how Mike got keys to my car, or my apartment. Monday morning I made a follow up call to the insurance company in Houston about my car being stolen. I still remember the license number was MQF 569. The lady put me on hold for someone in claims to help ASAP. When I heard the friendly voice, I said Harrison Ford is that you? He said Ron Adair, it has been a long time, how in the world are you? I had been his supervisor in Houston, when we both worked at Western and Southern Life Ins. Co. He was a black man, and a great friend. He helped me get my claim processed. I bought a reprocessed 17 passenger van that could help with church activities.

FYI, this van was used a lot while working with our church. About a year later, I got a call from the son of Mr. Jerry Jones, a dear friend who was very active in our church. The problem was, this son and two buddies had planned this tour for the summer. They had a van made available to them for this 5000 mile tour to Florida and the many states they would be going to. They had their own sound system, the various churches they would be singing and performing in, as well as homes to provide sleeping quarters. Our church had been helping with the planning for this summer trip, before they returned to go on to college. They left, got about 75 miles down the road and the transmission in that van broke down. His question, Mr. Adair, is there any possibility that your van could be used on such short notice, for such a trip as this? Yes, you can get it today, and I will look for it back when I see you coming. They were gone in it for three months, and had put over 5,000 miles on it. That van served my purpose for over three years, and I sold it for $1000 more than I had paid for it. I had put more than 35,000 miles on it myself.

Remember my stolen car? It was about this time that I received a call from the Longview Police Dept. They had found my stolen car. I asked about its condition, and the officer asked how long has it been stolen? I explained that my auto insurance had paid me for it over three years ago. I told the officer the license number MQF 569, he said that's it. He then explained that they had just been notified about it. He also told me that it was probably sold back and forth between other's like this "Mike". Where they use it till the wheels fall off. They use stolen tags, and inspection stickers off of junk cars, then the last one that has it when it is completely worn out just runs it into a river, or leaves it abandoned in a forest somewhere. He said right now, it is in Northern Arkansas. I thanked him, and told him the name of the insurance company that now owned that car.

Mobberly Baptist Youth Go To Hawaii

Another very good memory of being involved with this church was a trip to Hawaii. Our Minister of Music, Mr. Dale Perkins had always taken our Youth Choir on a field trip each year. They would go to some special place each third year. This trip to Hawaii was one of those "special places". Can you imagine any place better? OK, I do love TEXAS, but I had been to Hawaii while in the Navy Seabees. This would be a trip with memories for a life time. Approximately two hundred thirty five members of our youth choir, and fifty adults. The trip started off flying from Dallas Ft. Worth airport to Los Angeles, California. Dale had done his home work. He had the right travel agency, he had chartered buses, had made arrangements for the change of planes in Los Angeles, he had detailed planned places for the Youth Choir to sing, the transportation to our hotel, and when and where we would go, during this fantastic two week trip. The first slip up that I and all others became aware of was during our flight from Los Angeles. Dale had his Mother from Louisiana come on this trip with us. She was a real trooper, and we all just fell in love with her. She had been given the VIP escort of getting her to our connecting flight, while the rest of us walked to the gate and got on board the plane. We had been in the air for perhaps thirty minutes or so when Dale started looking to check on his Mom. She was not on board with any of us. The pilot called back to the airport and she had somehow been left behind. The pilot told Dale his Mother thought it was funny, and she was already on another flight to Hawaii.

The Dole Pineapple Factory was one of the planned stops for us to tour. We had so many going thru it that some of our folks were still in line when Jim Bob Ralls and I came out. We thought it would be fun to go thru it again, and take advantage of the sweets they made available to all of us. The third time was the charm, he and I had eaten several banana splits with the ice cream and pineapple on top. We had plenty of free time during this period where we could take advantage of other sweets so we did. I had my fill on the pineapple pie, pineapple cake, and malts. I was one happy camper till the next day when I had ulcers in my mouth from too much acid. It got better and better after drinking a lot of water.

Another day and another island one young man in our youth group came to me and asked for my help. He made the point, help was needed, but could I keep it a secret? His friend had hurt himself, but they did not want our pastor to know about the problem. There were several problems here, first I did want to help, but the help needed was serious. I asked this fellow his name, I knew him by his familiar first name, but I did not know his last name. When he told me it was Johnson, I was ok with that, like Jones, or Smith, but now several are explaining to me who he is. His dad is our Pastor, Dr. Laney Johnson, who is also on this trip with his caring wife and Mom to son number one.

Yes, number one son is the one that has this serious problem. We have to get their help.

FYI, on this trip we had to be careful. Dale had talked to us as a group, just the adults before this trip. This was not Dale Perkins first "RODEO", and just like all the trips, he warned us to be prepared for the unexpected. To step up when called upon, and if for whatever reason we needed help, or knew of a problem to be certain that the problem is TAKEN CARE OF, AND SOLVED. All of us knew that Dale and especially our Pastor, was available 24/7. Here was the problem, we got instructions every time we came to our destination. Sometimes, before anyone stepped off a bus, there were guidelines, or instructions of what was permitted, and most important WHAT NOT TO DO at "this" location. Here we were going to have some free time again to play on the beach, sun bathe, read, walk the beach, or just enjoy ourselves. WE WERE TOLD TO NOT EVEN THINK ABOUT CLIMBING THE PALM TREES. That some of them were growing on a low slant, and looked inviting to just walk on. This warning, as so many times, came from "our guide" that Dale had prearranged to help us have a good time. Another real danger, was to respect the under-tow in the waves coming upon the sandy beaches. Our pastors son was a "PK", "preacher's kid", and bless their hearts, the "PK's" just seem to be drawn into trouble. Would you agree? This "PK" knew better, but just had to prove "our guide" was wrong and did in fact attempt to climb one of these Palm Trees.

Remember the secret I was asked to keep? I was looking this young PK in the eyes, and saw such pain from all these, what looked like needles, sticking in both hands, his arms, and in his stomach. He had learned the hard way, that yes, you can see the natives climb a palm tree, and come down. What you do not do is try to come down like you would from a tree in your back yard. I saw he needed medical attention, not just someone's first aid. So, I had told his friends, and him, that he had a problem that was a lot more serious than just worrying about his dad. He was taken right then to the hospital, that did help him recover, but that took several days and everyone knew what had happened.

Dale Perkins is, and always has been a true KINDRED SPIRIT. I have loved this church, for its many, and various ministries. It was a pleasure to be part of the expansion, and move to the North side of town. The new location was to be on the loop, and build bigger, as the city of Longview was growing in every direction. We had some that volunteered to go teach Sunday School, in the school building to draw new folks into our "worship family". That worked out just fine, and with the promise of growing our church, the first building on our new property was a Gym, with a full kitchen. It was used as our worship center, and had petitions/or dividers for many class rooms.

FYI, Dale and wife Shirley Perkins have three sons and two daughters. Their three sons are leading music in different churches. Their second son Stacie is a friend and Minister of Music at Harmony Hill Baptist Church in Lufkin, Texas. Shirley Perkins received her heavenly reward on December 23, 2018 at the age of 82.

Another Gideon

Never Ending Jobs

I Joined the Gideon's International Organization in Longview, TX on August 6, 1981. That was 39 years ago as of August 2020. I have been a member in many cities over the years. The Lufkin West Camp is where I've served for twenty years now. My responsibilities as our Scripture Chairman are to line up distribution times and places, order bibles needed and store them. Mr. Marvin McDonald has furnished the storage space in his Huntington location. I first ask him to allow us to keep the bibles at no charge. He told me it was his pleasure to help the Gideon International Ministry. That has been almost twenty years now. We would meet every Saturday morning, at Lufkin's Golden Corral. Now, with the Covid 19 Pandemic we are meeting via conference calls. We read scripture for a few minutes then jot down those we need to be praying for. The list always includes our POLICE, LAW ENFORCEMENT, our MILITARY serving all over the world and their families. FIRST RESPONDERS, our PRESIDENT, ELECTED LEADERS, GIDEON'S MINISTRY, in over 200 countries. Also for our NURSES, DOCTORS, HOSPITALS, SCHOOLS, TEACHERS, STUDENTS, PASTORS, CHURCHES, the PRAYER LIST each church has and those churches looking for pastors and those pastors looking for churches. Then those on our hearts that we name. We pair up, each one of us gets on our knees and we pray for each of these on our hearts. This prayer time always includes the crisis at that time, in the world and at home.

Gideons are now in more than two hundred countries, all

over the world. Starting in 1898 when John Nicholson and Samuel Hill share a room and a vision. In 1899 Nicholson, Hill, and W.J. Knights, prayerfully choose a name: THE GIDEONS. A pastor, in 1908, proposes churches be responsible to raise funds for Bible placement by Gideons. 1916 Gideon Hospital Bible placements begin. 1934 Auxiliary supply Bibles to women's homes, hospitals, and Y.W.C.A.'s.

R. G. LeTourneau

1940 Mr. R. G. LeTourneau was elected international president. In 1946 he founded the LeTourneau College that I attended years later. 1941 The first New Testaments are distributed to military personnel. The Gideon Auxiliary begin distributions of New Testaments to service nurses. 1946 Gideons begin distributions to students in 5th - 12th grades. 1948 - 1955 The Netherlands, South Africa, Japan, and Ecuador are added. 1968 Service Testaments circle the moon in Apollo 8. In 1972 Distributions to college students are initiated. 1978 The 200 millionth Scripture is ordered. 1989 Poland, Hungary, and Yugoslavia are opened.

1990 The 500 millionth Scripture is ordered. 2001 The 1 billionth Scripture is ordered. 2008 GIDEONS CELEBRATE 100 YEARS OF DISTRIBUTING GOD'S WORD.

In 2015 the second billionth Scripture is ordered, and the Gideon Bible App is introduced. The 200th country, territory, or possession is opened: Saint Martin. 2016 Over 91.8 million Scriptures are shared - a new one year record. 2017 Total camps worldwide exceed 12,000 for the first time.

Once a year, we ask pastors to partner with us by allowing a certified Gideon speaker to address his church. We are asking them to donate over and above their tithe to help us buy bibles. One hundred percent of all donations go to pay for bibles and shipping.

Here in Lufkin we have two camps for Angelina County. The East Camp works East of Hwy. 59, and The West Camp works West of Hwy 59.

My best friend today is Jim Wilson age 80, legally-blind and active member in our Gideon East Camp with his wife Pat active in our Auxiliary, both are proud parents of their daughter Janna. Our Auxiliary are especially helpful in prayer support, as well as getting bibles to nurses as they graduate and where they work.

Jim Wilson's Testimony

Jim quotes his testimony as follows.

"My grandfather was a minister and was pastor for several churches during his career. He worked various jobs and did some farming as a young man. Occasionally, he would preach at a country church when asked to do so. As he continued to fill pulpits, he felt God's call on his life to preach. He was married and had four children when he attended seminary. He was always teasing family members. He loved to fish in the lake or river as well as being a fisherman for men. Whenever he went fishing, he always brought home fish to be cooked. If the fish weren't biting, he would stop by the fish market to purchase some. He would always say, 'We Got Some!'

When my mother was eight years old and her younger brother was six, my grandparents were gone to a ministerial conference and left them and their toddler twin brother and sister in the care of a caretaker. She and my uncle decided to drive the family vehicle across town to visit some family friends. My mother held a baby on each knee as my uncle drove the car. They threatened their caregiver not to tell. She didn't have to worry, the friends tattled on them. They came by their mischievousness' honestly.

My parents divorced when I was about nine years old. I was an only child. Divorce is a tramatic experience for children because we love both parents. It is an experience that is difficult to explain to young children. Both remarried about a year later. I spent quite a bit of time with my grandparents when I was growing up and they influenced me greatly. I even lived with them when my parents first divorced and then another year or so when I was attending high school. After high school graduation, I joined the United States Marines. During the time I was in the Marine Corps, I was attracted by the world and did some things that I regret. I had gone forward to accept Christ as my Savior when I was six years old and even baptized by my grandfather.

After serving with the Marines, I worked as a nurse and orderly at Denton State school for a while. There was a little ten year old cerebral palsy girl there whose parents had rejected, because she was so twisted. We had to literally tie her into the wheel chair with sheets to keep her from falling out. She would ask me to tuck her into bed each night and then asked me to read to her from a Gideon Bible. After a few nights of reading to her, God began to touch my heart. I heard Him say to me, "You once loved me and had fellowship with me. Is the world really that appealing?

I began to realize that if a little girl so twisted and dependent on others could love God, why didn't I? I had so much for which to be thankful. I'm sure there were many prayers offered on my behalf from my Godly grandparents. Thankfully, I rededicated my life to Him and now am a Gideon member. I work to help with distributions of Gideon Bibles and speak in churches about the Gideon Ministry. After my dad remarried, he and my stepmother brought a sister and a brother into my life. Ironically, my younger brother is responsible for introducing me to the Gideon Ministry."

Thank you Jim for your testimony, and being my best friend.

We hand out bibles to the fifth graders, to colleges, to hotels, nursing homes, funeral homes, offices, and all kinds of festivals. Some of these include the Cinco de Mayo, Tamale, VFW, and Catfish festivals. When we do a college, we invite other camps in towns several hours away to come help us distribute the green New Testament. Here our Angelina College is located in Lufkin, Texas. The Gideon's distributed over 2500 bibles there in 2019. We do this after Easter, from 7 am to 7 pm all day long. The bibles we hand out are free. They are paid for by the gifts from churches we partner with to help put a bible into the hands of those local, and around the world. Gideon Corporate Head Quarters are in Nashville, Tennessee. "*Sowers Of The Word*" is a 95 year history of the Gideons. They have just made another updated NEW history book "*Witness To History*" that is available. Serving with the Gideons is a real blessing. Please keep the Gideon Ministry in your prayers.

SALUTE to recent Gideon members

I SALUTE those faithful Gideons from Angelina county that have gone on to be with our Lord. Some of these include:

In the East Camp... Mr. Jim Reagan, Scripture Chairman, and Church Ministry Chairman. Faithful and loved by us all.

In the West Camp... Mr. Richard Alexander, Scripture Chairman

Mr. Robert Roberson, Church Ministry Chairman

Mr. Dave Winfrey, very faithful and active member

Dr. Russell Ingram, very faithful supporter

Mr. Kenneth McGee, was a very active member

Mr. Vernon Horton, Faith Fund Chairman and assistant to Scripture Chairman

Mrs. Elizabeth Lee, Auxiliary Camp President

Mr. Andy Modesitte, an active faithful member

Mr. Constantino Villasana, a faithful member

Mr. Dan Lamont, a faithful member

The GIDEON MINISTRY is all about winning souls for Christ. Yes, we hand out bibles, because God blesses His word.

Isaiah 55:11 So shall my word be that goeth forth out of my mouth: it shall not return unto me void, but it shall accomplish that which I please, and it shall prosper in the thing whereto I sent it. (KJV)

Another Consulting Opportunity

Job # 16 CXI Corporation

1982 Consulting work for CXI, Sargent Oil and Gas, Texas Lignite Corp.

Dave's downtown property and other projects were part of my work load. He called me to put on my truck driving hat when he let some drivers go, due to their not passing a surprise drug test. He had his own fleet of KW's (Kenworth) 18 wheelers. I agreed to drive one of his tanker trucks for 30 to 90 days, until he could get fresh new replacement drivers.

On another project, he sent me with Mr. Bob Kautzman, to go explore some coal tailings located on the state borders of Missouri and Kansas. It was in the dead of winter, 1982. Cold weather is really hard on me. We drove my company Ford Bronco there in the snow, it had four wheel drive. Driving to our destination my left tires were in Kansas, while the right tires were in Missouri, on this state line country road. We walked out onto frozen "holding ponds" that were full of coal tailings. We drove 4" PVC pipe down ten feet or more thru the ice. Then we used an auger to dig down into that PVC pipe, removing the coal tailings a few feet at a time to get the needed "samples". It was a rather tedious job while snowing and about 10 degrees. There was a large barn nearby with heaters going and men were working inside. That was a life saver. When we took a lunch break, we drove on north a ways to a restaurant. They had food like Mom would fix. I was so cold, my face looked like an invisible person was using both hands to massage it. Kautzman asked me if I was ok. NO!! I had winter clothes on but that experience was the coldest day of my life. I ate a plate lunch with chicken fried steak, mashed potatoes and gravy, corn, green beans and cornbread. It helped thaw me out, so I asked for the same thing again, and ate that too. That experience was so VERY COLD!

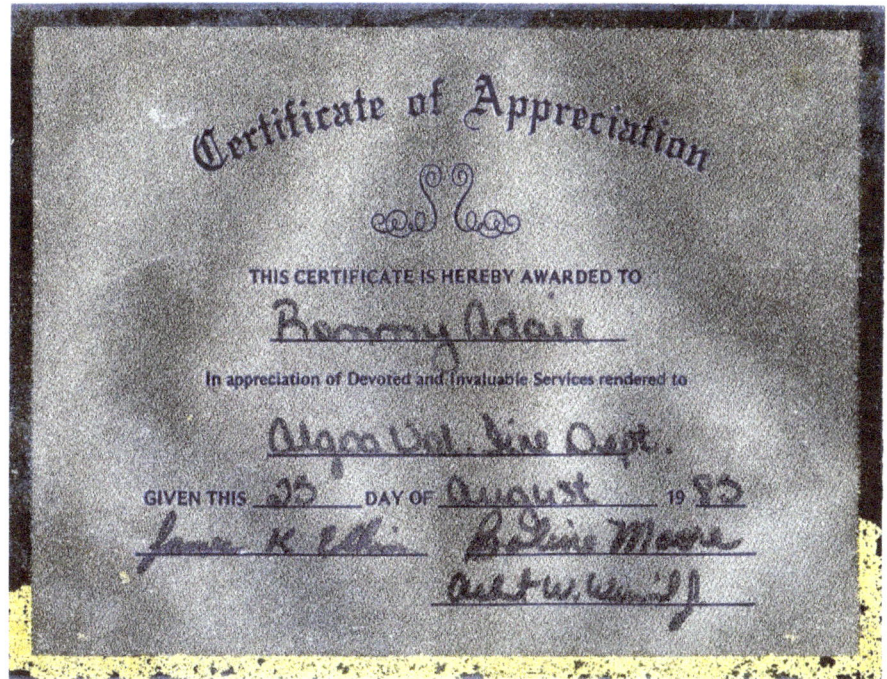

Appreciation for many years service Vol. Fireman

Job # 17 CXI in Terre Haute, Indiana

February 9, 1983 Dave sent me to Terre Haute, Indiana on a project that one of his companies was retrieving coal tailings from an old holding pond. These coal fragments were dried, then I would check the sulfur content for quality control. This was then sold to be mixed with coal that was mined in that area. This required about 12 other employees. My job was to monitor the activity or progress, and run the quality control lab. Then reports were made by phone to Mr. Les Moore and Mr. Dave Smith in our CXI office in Houston. We built a large building to house the operation. The project manager was almost killed one day.

(See A.N.D.E. Volume 2 for details.)

This area of Indiana reminds me of good old E. TX, with the rolling hills, and trees, it is all so beautiful. The county just North of Terre Haute is named Park County, for the many covered bridges. There were about 35, but some have been lost due to various problems. Like folks camping in or near one and having a camp fire inside, causing the bridge to be burned up. These are very special to me. The heavy timbers that they are made of and the beautiful setting with the water below, and country-side beauty. It is breath taking to drive, or walk thru. On the second week-end in October each year the county roads become one way for the covered bridge festival with thousands of folks enjoying all these special wonders. For those living in that area it must me a nightmare trying to go see a neighbor, go to town, or just go period. They have to go one way all the way around the area to get back home. Thousands and thousands of folks like me just love those covered bridges, and come here to see them.

A Southern Baptist Church I found there was the Sandy Creek Baptist Church on the West side of Terra Haute. Our Lord knows our heart, and wants us to make the best of our life. Do you really like your work and enjoy what you do? What are some of the "things" you like to collect, or do in your own spare time? I have had many friends thru the years, some like to collect stamps, coins, keys, pictures of cats, dogs, barns and well you see where I'm headed. Almost forgot Mrs. Brawner, lived near Dickinson, Texas she collected pot holders. She and her husband were my folks very close friends. They had a son Terry about 15 years younger than me, and his younger sister named Jackie. I like covered bridges, kind of hard to collect them. Things made of heavy, thick, wood, is my hot button, that is what the covered bridges are made of. Most of them are a hundred years old, or older. After church, and lunch, every Sunday, would find me going to see more of these beauties.

Job # 18 Sales Representative

0/83-09/84 Sale Electric Supply Co. Longview, Sales Rep. for Mgr. Mr. Gene Gunnels.

While my knowledge of the electrical field was really limited, I've always enjoyed meeting people. For me to call on electrical contractors, home builders, construction companies, etc. was comfortable for me. When a potential customer had a question I could not answer, I would give our Longview office a call and my support team would help make that sale and delivery. Electricity is the one thing I personally do not even try to tinker with. It is always best left to the experts who know what they are doing. My dad taught me a lot about it. We ran conduit pipe to protect the wires in all the buildings we built, which include a large truck barn, tractor sheds, workshops, two story garage apartment and more. I do not work with electricity.

Job # 19, Hydrotex, Inc. Dallas, TX

09/84-12/84 Sales Rep. for high performance lubricants.

They all smoked. My first salesmen meeting in Dallas was in a room full of smoke. I asked the Regional Manager when they were going to stop smoking so the room could clear from all the smoke. He said, as he took another puff on his cigar, that they always smoke during their meetings. Little did I know about this "got-cha". When I interviewed for the job, and was hired, their office had no ash-trays. No one smelled of smoke.

My sales kit was left on their table, with a note, "Thanks, but I do not smoke"! Adair and Sons had used their products and a competitor, Catus. We knew they were top of the line. CXI, in Houston, LeTourneau Mfg. in Longview, and Sabine Mining in Marshall are just a few of the larger companies my sales efforts helped. I really liked selling for them.

One of the sales pitches we used was to put a hand full of MT-155 grease on a block of wood and strike it with a sledge hammer. The customer would see what I was doing in their shop with their sledge hammer. They would put their hand and arm up quickly to protect their eyes, as they turned their back toward me. Most any other lubricants would splatter and make a mess covering 10 to 15 feet in all directions. Not Hydrotex, this grease was heat, dirt and water resistant. It stayed on the sledge hammer and wood only. I'd use some paper towels to clean the hammer and wood. This fact and a little information would make sale after sale. We sold transmission fluid to trucking companies, to schools for their bus fleet, and to cities for the fire trucks, police cars, etc. It really did extend the life of the transmissions. It was fun and I enjoyed my work!!

Job # 20 CXI Consultant

12/84-08/86 Sergeant Oil and Gas.

Again, Mr. Dave Smith, wanted my assistance to help one of his companies, Sergeant Oil and Gas. His CEO, was Mr. Joe Durrett with associates, Mr. John Orhood and others that I had worked with before. Some of this work was in Houston, Galena Park, Baytown, Pasadena, downtown and in Longview, TX. Work would also include his "bell project" from time to time.

Dave certainly got a great pleasure giving a bell away to some very deserving person or company. He gave to policemen, small new churches, pastors, someone he felt was doing a great job, employees after years of service, University professors, and the list goes on. This too, was a true labor of love.

FYI, Since June, 1971, I've sold life insurance to present date. I have always been active in church work. In 1985, I was back in Houston and now a member of the Second Baptist Church, where Dr. Ed Young was the pastor. Many of my friends at SMBC, had moved to this church and it was also growing in a great way. I have always loved Houston, because of its love of people. It makes no difference what color our skin is, or the vocation we work at. The churches of Houston welcome you, and accept you just as you are. We all have only one true God, and I'm thankful that He looks at the heart, and knows our Soul. I do love people, I look forward to going to church, to be able to sing songs of praise, and to be a part of the worship service. For the Pastor to open the Bible, read a portion, and encourage each one of us to do better than we have done. To appreciate the way our Lord has, and is working in each of our lives. THAT IS WHAT THIS BOOK IS ALL ABOUT. Ron Adair has been so richly blessed. Please know this, I'm praying for you. How do you want your life to end? What has our Lord done in your life. No matter your age, skills, or past history, we are still here. Help me make our world a better and safer place to live for Him. Let Him come into your heart if he is not there already. His Holy Spirit will guide and help you the rest of your life. Me, "I just want to end well". Have a blessed day, and if you dare, or care to, read on.

Another Business LADD

Job # 21 Landscape Additions

08/86 - 08/87 In 1986 the great job I had with CXI, came to an end. CXI was going through some trying times, and economic setbacks. A friend contacted me, and told me he knew of a great job opportunity with some of his friends. I drove to North Houston, and met these friends from Utah, at the Marriot Hotel near the Houston Intercontinental Air Port. This new job sounded good, looked good, and felt good. I'm telling my friend from church about the new job, and he is still telling me to call BJ, and just have lunch, or buy her a hamburger. I'm not calling her, got my hands full trying to make a living.

This job opportunity, was to start my own landscaping business, and do it here in Longview. This friend helped me get started with what savings I had, and a few friends investing in me. This was a true struggle, trying to make my monthly expenses, and start up a new business. Friends from church paid my house note, more than just a few times. Some of his friends knew I was struggling, and invited me to come on out to Utah. They promised me I could work with them for a few weeks, then go on to work in California where they had crews working. They told me they have a friend that is working out of town for a few months. I could stay in his home, and save money, not having to pay for motel or lodging. All I had to do was get there. I told my church friends, and a few others. Packed up and drove my 1980 Ford four-wheel drive Bronco to Salt Lake City, Utah.

They did have the work crews and work to do. I got located in this friends big fancy home, using one guest bedroom, and bath/shower. Worked long and hard for the first four days, then found out that I needed to get a motel or place to stay. The friend with the fine home was coming back, and I needed to make other arrangements.

I looked in the phone book for a Southern Baptist Church, when I first came into town. This was Thursday evening, they told me to find another place to sleep. That was the first slap in the face, so to speak. I did not know if I would find anyone at this Baptist Church, but it did have SBC (Southern Baptist Convention), on the Yellow Page, by the Ph. number. Most all I had ever known in the churches I attended were "SBC". When I got there, it was about an hour, or more before dark. A crew of men were working there. They were adding on another building to the church. I talked to the pastor, and explained my situation. I had no money for motel, I could charge it to my credit card but I really did not want to do that. I thought perhaps an older couple in the church might have a spare room, for about a week or so, that I could rent cheap.

The pastor took me around to the crew chief and asked him if the workers could put up with an intruder for a week or so. The church had cots, sheets, blanket, and I could share the showers. This was great, I promised them I would stay a day or two to help them with their project, once I had mine under-control.

These friends I met in Houston really took more than full advantage of me. I was the first, or at least one of the first to be on the job every day. Starting about 6am and working till about 7 to 8pm each day Monday thru Saturday, and now toward the end of my first week, as we were finishing Saturday evening, they asked me to help on Sunday. It seemed that the Manager of Sears had only Sunday to get his new home landscaped.

I was told a crew would be working on it, and when they got finished, they would call it a day. That next day, Sunday, the crew was one fellow who was running a crew and going on out to California in another week or two. He had a helper that was going to work with me. It was just three of us, doing the work of six or more, on this special over-time job. We did it, and finished about 9pm. On Monday, Tuesday, Wednesday, Thursday,

Friday, and Saturday it was thirteen, or more hours each day. They just kept on telling me what a great help I was, and doing such a great job. Now late Saturday afternoon, they gave me by pay check for the two weeks of hard work. It was less than $200. I asked how they came up with that number, and did they not have any concern for doing what is right? My total hours over the two weeks, fourteen straight days, with an average of over 12 hours per day, was 168 hours. They paid me less than $1.20 per hour. This injustice was in part my fault. You see, I told them to pay me whatever they felt was right. Some folks will take advantage of you, I knew that.

    I did stay at the church. Enjoyed the Sunday services, and worked on the church Monday. Tuesday morning all the workers gave me a hearty hand shake, and told me to get on back to Texas, and see what the Good Lord has in store for me. I felt so tired, disappointed, broken, and broke. I drove to a rest area just South of Amarillo, Texas. Slept in my Bronco, got up, and my truck would not even try to start. A big-rig truck driver walked over to help. We both agreed, it had to be the starter. He gave me a ride to the next town. He went into the auto supply with me, and promised to get me a trucker going back my way. The folks in the auto supply told the trucker, to not worry, they would give me a ride back, and make sure the starter was the problem. The starter installed, and road service, was all about $75. I was on the road again, and made it back home the next night.

    I was really tired when I laid down on my bed, and the phone rang. It was Bettie Jane Nelson (BJ), the twice divorced lady from Mt. Vernon. She understood how tired and disappointed I was. We talked for about an hour on the phone. It was a few days later, when we did go out to eat.

Another Insurance A.L. Williams

Job # 22, A.L. Williams Insurance

10/87-07/88 A. L. Williams Insurance Longview, TX. Sales throughout East Texas areas.

This company was of interest to me because Mr. A. L. Williams took on the whole life insurance industry. He went against the normal way life insurance was sold. He was a very successful football coach. He was recruited to sell life insurance during the summer to earn a few extra dollars. He was taught what to do, how to sell insurance, and the difference between "whole life insurance" and "term" insurance. Right away, he saw some flaws with certain insurance companies and the way some agents sold the insurance. I, for one, salute anyone who stands their ground and tries to be counted in the cause of "RIGHT"!! Mr. Williams was taken to court and lost his license to sell insurance. Quite a scandal took place. The bottom line is this. He won!!! For the first time in the history of life insurance, all insurance companies had to re-think their sales approach and options. Mr. A.L Williams with his trusted attorneys and financial investment folks proved to the courts there was a better way to sell life insurance. Yes, he rocked the boat. He kept his license to sell insurance, quit his job coaching football, and went on to be a multi-millionaire with his own insurance company. He did good, for the insurance industry all over the world. To those like him, I say again, LEAD ON!

It was good to be back in Longview, and once again a member of Mobberly Ave. Baptist Church. Times were hard, and many folks were laid off, including myself, or lost their jobs because of cut backs, due to companies trying to just survive, and reducing their work force.

Another Drive Through Backwards

Norma Patrick

About March 1988.

One Sunday after church a great lady friend, Norma Patrick and I went out to eat. We were going to Luby's Cafeteria. She said, let's just go to McDonalds drive through. I explained that I do not go to any drive through, fast food service. She was insisting, so I explained that I do not talk to "POST" or "WALLS". Those two-way speakers were not put there for me. We were almost to the McDonalds when I gave in, and said OK, but we will do it my way.

I got in line to go thru, and she said what are you doing? We were looking at the line of cars in front of us. The cars in front of us were actually waiting their turn behind us, because I had pulled in, and turned around. Now I was in line BACKWARDS, so she could talk to the post or wall to place her order. She could not believe this was happening, but it did. We never went thru a drive thru again.

FYI, now it is July of 2020 and the world has been hammered by the Covid-19, virus. For more than a 120 days I have been going to more "drive up windows " than I can count. Calling in my food orders to go, then going to the drive-thru. Never say "never".

Another Challenge MasterGuard

Job #23 MasterGuard

07/88 - 09/89 A MasterGuard Sales Rep. for residential fire protection selling both smoke and heat detectors. Safety and saving lives, has always been and will always be, very dear to my heart. We need to help one another and be on the lookout for situations around us all the time, that may cause harm to us or someone else. We did not use scare tactics or pressure. In all my years of selling various items or services, I've always tried to satisfy a need. Many times there may be a "REAL NEED" but if the potential customer does not see it, feel it, know or understand it, I just tell myself "NEXT" and move on. Many times folks just could not afford to buy our products. This is a "must have" product and I would encourage them to contact their local fire department for items like ours that were cheaper or free. Having been a volunteer fireman, (VFD) member and knowing the dangers of fire, this too, was not hard to sell. Fires start so easily and often without warning.

On this subject, may I ask you? Do you have fire insurance on your own life? Point is, I've sold life insurance to help loved ones be prepared to help their family when they or another member dies. The FIRE ASSURANCE I'm speaking of here, is that of knowing when you die, you will wake up in heaven. This insurance policy and assurance is absolutely free."Paid In Full", by our Lord and Savior, Jesus Christ. Do you have this peace of mind in your heart? If so, GREAT. IF NOT, please know you can have this all knowing and comforting peace, right now. First Corinthians 15: 1-4

THANK YOU LORD!

Another Marriage / Second Time

Second Wife

August 28, 1988 Married my second wife, Bettie Jane Nelson from Talco, Texas. Her last husband F.J.N. and I were attending a bible study class in Longview. We went to lunch together many times after church. He had told me his marriage was on the rocks, and they would probably be going through a divorce.

We always prayed before eating. This prayer always included our asking the Lord to work in our lives, and thanking Him for helping us in our several needs. I understood BJ was his second wife, for the second time. He and BJ were married before, then divorced, and again remarried her the second time. He had talked for several months to BJ about his prayer partner at church. One Sunday he told me they would like me to come have lunch with them, but beware of BJ's dog Solo.

Ron, wife Bettie Jane, and Solo at home in Longview, TX

Several weeks later, I did have lunch, and a good visit with them, and met her Austrailian Shepard, part Catahola, dog named Solo. His youngest son was a senior and still in school. BJ was not able to get along with him at all. I was shown the deep groves his son carved into the wood arm rest on BJ's favorite Lazy-boy recliner. They asked me if one of my bedrooms could be rented out, so his son could stay in the same school district.

If they could just get him out from under their roof till he graduates, and moves on with his life, perhaps they could have a life also. My response was that he would have to follow my rules. I agreed to meet him, and his father at my four bedroom home to discuss the possibilities. Thanks were given for a fine home cooked meal, and I left.

When he and his son came to my home the young man seemed to be polite and agreed to all my rules. For the next 90 days, until he graduates he must keep focused and disciplined. He was on probation, there would be no second chance. One strike and you are out. He and his dad had a copy of my rules: He would not cook, he could bring "fast-food" in, but eat it at the kitchen table only. He could not have any visitors on my property period. He could not work on his car here.

The first thirty days flew by with no problems. He had his own car, and drove to and from school. When I came home one day about 2:30 in the afternoon, his car was there. When I went in there were two voices, so I walked on past his room, to my bedroom. His door was wide open, and they were making love on his bed, but did not notice me either time as I walked back out to the kitchen. I opened and closed the door to the garage. Then I announced that "I'm home", he said "I'll be right out."

He was but she wasn't, so we just small talked as he told me he had to leave. I kept watch on my windows as we talked, and I could also see his car. He got in his car and was starting down my drive-way when I walked out to stop him. Hello young lady, I don't think we have been introduced. She had gone out the window and ducked low to rush to his car, and I did not see her, until I stopped his leaving. He was told to go ahead, but don't come back for three days, and then only if his dad was with him. Your room will be just like you left it. A locksmith came on out and changed my locks with new keys.

His dad called about getting his things, and moving out. I have not seen his son since. Often we would still go out to eat after church. Six months later he tells me that the second divorce with BJ is final. Several more months go by and he keeps telling me to call BJ.

He knew I had gone to Salt Lake City, Utah. He also knew it was a great disappointment, and I was coming home. That is when BJ called me, and we talked about an hour. We kept in touch as I was looking for a regular job, and started working for MasterGuard of Longview.

BJ and I dated for several months and decided to get married. This would be my second marriage, and second wife. However, for BJ, this would be her fifth marriage, and I would be the third man in her life. She married and divorced her first husband "twice". Then did the same with friend F.J.N., married and divorced "twice". I explained to BJ that she would only have one marriage with me. If and when that comes to an end, she would not have a re-do on Ron Adair.

We had been married for a year, as I worked with Masterguard. Our company was having a convention in Dallas in Sept. of 1989. BJ and I drove my Ford Bronco to the Dallas convention, but broke down just a few blocks from our hotel. We caught a cab to the hotel, got registered for both the rooms and the convention. When I explained our situation to our Mgr. in Longview, (my boss), Mr. Gene Shelton, said his Cadillac was parked in the hotel covered parking and would cost so much to take out and return. Besides he said, I do not want to take a chance of missing any of the convention. I'm thinking HEY, it starts tomorrow, but I simply said, OK, I will figure something out.

I talked to the "BELL CAPTAIN" about my problem, and he said come to my office, we can help you sir. He flips thru his card file and gives me the name of several reliable repair shops that could help. The first one I called seemed supportive, and understanding. He said they would come by our hotel and get me to go with them to my truck. They did not charge for a tow and were very fair on the repairs. Our ride was ready before the convention was over. BJ and I left the convention early because I was anxious to find a friendly employer. Life is short, to not help someone in need is a shame.

BJ was always supportive in my decisions, and I had a hard time with this one. I had bought my new four bedroom home in 1979. Had paid notes for over ten years, but it was hard to keep going. Our Lord allows things to happen that we fail to understand. While working thru the options as we saw them, we took a step of faith and moved out of my home.

First Baptist Church Mt. Vernon, Texas found me joining there with my second wife Bettie Jane Nelson Adair. She had a home place about ten miles to the North, near Hagansport. I helped do some home repairs on her place, and we lived there for about thirteen years. I do not recall how long we were members of the Mt. Vernon church, but we did move our membership to the Mt. Olive Baptist Church in Hagansport. Our Pastor there was Randy Sinclair. He worked as an Adult Probation Officer in the counties nearby. His wife was a great school teacher, she loved kids. We only had a few kids in our church, but there were twenty or more kids with in a four mile area. Bettie Jane and I were asked if we would take on the job of building a youth group, and teaching that class. The church had several special called meetings during the next several months, that were on odd days, so we did not take up "church" time trying to plan, and promote the project. Everyone was visiting, inviting, and encouraging folks to come to Mt. Olive Baptist Church. Several Adults said they would go get the kids, just let them know who needed a ride.

Pastor Randy and I visited together in most every home within three miles of our church. Bettie Jane (BJ) and I also did a lot of follow up visits together. The Lord helped our church grow in numbers, spiritually, and economically. BJ and I had gotten (her) a new used car, it was a Lincoln Towncar. It was blue and beautiful, and we took it down muddy driveways to pick up kids, and BJ did not mind a bit. I tried to keep it looking good. We made some long trips in it, and it was so dependable. The kids wore out the window motors in the back seat, but she did not mind a bit. Being the Youth Minister at that church was so rewarding in many ways. Mr. R.Q Tower's wife was such a tremendous help with the young girls. Several years later she died of cancer. That was a great loss to our neighborhood, and church. I just remembered R.Q. and I both have birthdays on February the 9th. He is five or six years older than me, but a great friend to us all. A friend told me about the construction of a new lake 20 miles NW near Cooper, TX.

Job # 24 Heavy Equipment Operator

09/89-12/89 LUHR Brothers Columbia, IL.

The manager liked to hire skilled veterans. When he understood my background in construction and the Seabees, he took me out to where the many scrapers were working. We watched several go by, then he said follow me. He stepped out into the roadway and flagged one of the newest machines down. He told me "OK, this is your ride, just remember the unit's number and have a nice day."He took that operator and put him on a different piece of equipment. I was one happy camper, working as a "Heavy Equipment Operator" on this new Cooper Lake Project. Operating a scraper that had a cab, heater and air conditioner, and moving clay to build this "Lake Cooper".

It was located eleven miles North of Sulphur Springs, TX. This project was enormous when completed in 1990, the lake covered almost 23,000 acres. September through December, was my time on this job. There were some cold mornings and days with bad weather to boot, at times. There was one younger black man that really took issue with my just starting on the job, and getting an almost new machine. He did, along with everyone else, have seniority over me. His scraper, like most all of the others, was open top. It had no cab, no heater, no air conditioner and it was an older, more wore out machine.

Bettie Jane was told that Mays Wholesale had an opening for a route salesman. This was in December and really cold, even with a cab and heater on my machine. The route salesman job was mine for the taking and I took it. Thank You Lord.

Job # 25 Truck Driver and Salesman

12/89-12/91 Mays Wholesale Mt. Vernon, TX

Bettie Jane told me about Mays Wholesale in Mt. Vernon, might have a job available. It would be driving a truck, and some days away from home. It had better pay, benefits, and was less than ten miles from home. I talked to the manager, and he hired me. Their headquarters were in Huntsville, Alabama, and they shipped truck loads of supplies to the Mt. Vernon terminal. They had nine trucks running routes out of the Mt. Vernon Hub. Each truck had a route to cover each day of the week, and if the route was close enough, you could come back to Mt. Vernon each night. There were days, and some weeks that you would stay in a motel to continue your route.

It was a good job, and BJ wanted to quit working for Dr. Miller, and go with me on the road. (FYI, Dr. Miller was getting older.) My route started the first week, working in and round Mt. Pleasant, and East Texas area. Got to go home most every night, and home most week-ends. On Saturday we would load up again, and go a little farther into the hill country, to Waco, and West Texas. We would drive back in, and load up again. This time we would drive to New Mexico, and Arizona. We were selling supplies to flower shops. They were already customers, expecting us on a certain day and at a certain time. They would call in orders to Mt. Vernon, so we would have those special supplies, plus whatever else they needed from our usual supply. BJ started going with me after I had been running the route many months.

Betty Jane does not like to be off the ground. She hates to go over any bridge. We had a picnic lunch to go, and stopped at a park to eat. Parking was on one side of this creek, with a wide bridge to walk across on to get to the tables on the other side. I carried the lunch, and walked slowly beside her while she went across on her hands and knees, but we got there. It was a good picnic, and we did get back across. On the road again, bad weather caught us coming back from Arizona, and New Mexico on one trip. We stopped in the Midland, and Odessa, Texas area. Got a motel room, and I got some sleep before trying to go on in this snow and ice. Later, when we did get back on the interstate, it was still snow and ice. The snow was so heavy, it was building up on the air intake above the back of our Peterbuilt Truck. I would have to find a safe place to pull off the road, usually an exit ramp, so I could get back on. I would get it cleaned off, but an hour or so later we would have to do it all over again. Eight hours later we were getting closer to home. We had less snow, and could keep on going slowly, still driving on ice and snow. We were both glad to be home.

Job # 26 Sales Representative

12/91-09/92 KBUS Radio Station Paris, TX

Sales Rep. in the North East Texas area from Texarkana to Dallas and North into Oklahoma. Then South to Sulphur Springs. Their office in Paris was forty miles from home. This work had a little different twist to it and working with the fun DJ's was something special every day. Calling on businesses to advertise on the radio was interesting work. It was good to be home every night.

I had worked on this job at the radio station for about nine months. One evening a call came from a friend, with a job offer from Houston.

Job # 27 Sales Representative

09/92-12/93 STASCO, Houston, TX

Sales Rep. in TX and Louisiana selling emergency lighting and safety equipment. They provided a pickup to drive. It was rigged out with flashing light bar and many of the different lights available. We also sold large truck tires, mud flaps and batteries of all shapes and sizes, etc. As I would come into a city, I'd locate their library. It would be a temporary office to locate the many places to call on. One sales call would be to the city garage. They maintained all the city cars and trucks. Another stop would be the bus barn for the school buses; they used a lot of emergency lights. I would also contact construction companies. They used a lot of safety equipment, fire extinguishers, batteries, etc. I would also contact both the fire and police departments.

Ron Adair is STASCO's emergency lighting and safety products specialist in east Texas and Louisiana.

This was a family owned business since 1945. It included Mr. Larry McGinty, his brother, Ken and their dad J.W. They sold supplies and tires to Adair & Sons since 1948. So yes, we had met, before I sold for them. They were a very dependable company and family. Thank You Lord.

It was about this time when BJ told me she wanted to get some geese to raise. We had the room with pastures on three sides, North, East, and West of our house. Her brother Gary had a large garden area with peas, or potatoes, on our South side, with an apple orchard nearby. They also had a peach orchard in that area. Just on our North side was a small pond for their cows. Back of our house about 100 yards was a large pond that we knew the geese would love. We placed the order for 12 geese, and paid in advance. We got them a few weeks later. Baby chicks, that we would raise, and take care of. My work with STASCO found me home most every night. These geese grew fast, as I had kept making their living space larger.

BJ started giving them names to match their personalities. One was a female, she called Miss Priss. Another was larger than the others, named Biggen. The one that followed me where ever I was, she named Pal. When I was outside, Pal was at my side. We both got a great deal of loving from these new friends.

STASCO thanked me, as that job came to a happy ending about 15 months later. It was time to move on. An ad in the newspaper for a salesman at the Ford Dealer in Mt. Pleasant came to my attention.

Job # 28, Auto Salesman

12/93-07/94 Donnie Keck Ford Mt. Pleasant

Auto sales of new, or used, cars and trucks in this area of East

Texas and loving it. After about four months, their top salesman was yours truly. It is a pleasure to help folks get something they need.

Whatever I do, the integrity has to be there. I sold a brand new pick-up to a man and his wife. The next day, he is not a happy camper. He tells me to go look at the top of his truck. I could not believe what I was seeing, duck tape covering three holes. With the tape off, the center hole was the size of a tennis ball. The other two were the size of a golf ball. This truck had been used and abused. Proper repairs were made, while the folks used another vehicle. Little did I know that Mr. Keck had relatives that used our new vehicles in their logging, and cattle business.

One beautiful day this old clunker of a pick-up comes up, leaving a smoke trail. The other salesmen were moving toward the back, and break room, before I noticed the old truck pull up. I walked on out, and greeted the older fellow dressed in over-alls. He told me he was here to buy his wife a new car. I just made a sweep of my arm and hand slowly, asking which car lot did he want to go look at first? We had them in front, and on both sides of the building, with more on the show room floor. He walked around me, so I opened the front door for him. He said let's look in here first. He went straight to the most expensive car we had on the property. It was a beautiful dark blue Continental Mark eight. It had more bells, and whistles, than I could tell him about, and that is just what I told him. This was in 1994, and this car had a hands-free phone that would respond to the owners voice only. The owner could say "call home", and it would be ringing. When the person on the other end answered hello, you just start talking till you say "by".

This was the car he wanted, and he told me he would bring

his wife in tomorrow. They had a car three years older like this one, and they would like to trade it in on the new one. He said, you tell your sales manager, that I want to make just one easy payment. For him to call Ford Motor Credit, that he would get the car tomorrow. Get it ready to drive out. Tell Ford Motor Credit Corporation, I will pay for the car in full, in six months. Go ahead and tell your sales manager. Well, by now there had been quite a buzz going around, and even Mr. Donnie Keck, Owner himself came out to greet this buyer, with the sales manager in tow. Mr. Keck stepped in front of me, to be in front of Mr. Worn-out overalls, when the older polite man said, excuse me sir, but this young man right here is my salesman. He is just asking that the sales manager call Ford Credit and assure your dealership that my word is my bond. Now do it, kind sir, please. The sales manager came back and told Mr. Donnie Keck that Ford Motor Credit, said he can buy every car, and truck we have on the property. The proud owner of the new dark blue car, left as a happy camper, in his old pick-up, with the smoke trail. The policy at our dealership was this. When a salesman takes another vehicle in on trade, that he has the first right to buy it, and or sell it, and be paid a fair commission for services rendered. That did not happen for me. The dealership sold this man's trade in to a "friend" of theirs. It is my opinion, that my honesty is what got me "fired" in July, 1994. Never been "fired" before. But it did happen again, several years later, and again for being "honest".

Job # 29, Insurance Sales

07/94-12/94 Marketing and Management Corp. of America, Paris, TX Life Ins. sales full time all over Texas and enjoying every day. Thank You Lord.

Job # 30, Insurance Sales

12/94-02/98 American National Ins., HQ. Galveston

Working out of their Tyler Office, but assigned to a "debit" which is a protected market area for their field Representative. In this case, for me, it was Henderson, TX, and that area. The company Sales Representative is responsible for servicing those customers that already have Ins. with that company. Another term for working like this is called a "captured" agent. They can only sell their insurance policies that are available. In other words, I could not sell for Great Southern Life Ins. Co. or any other, except American National Ins.

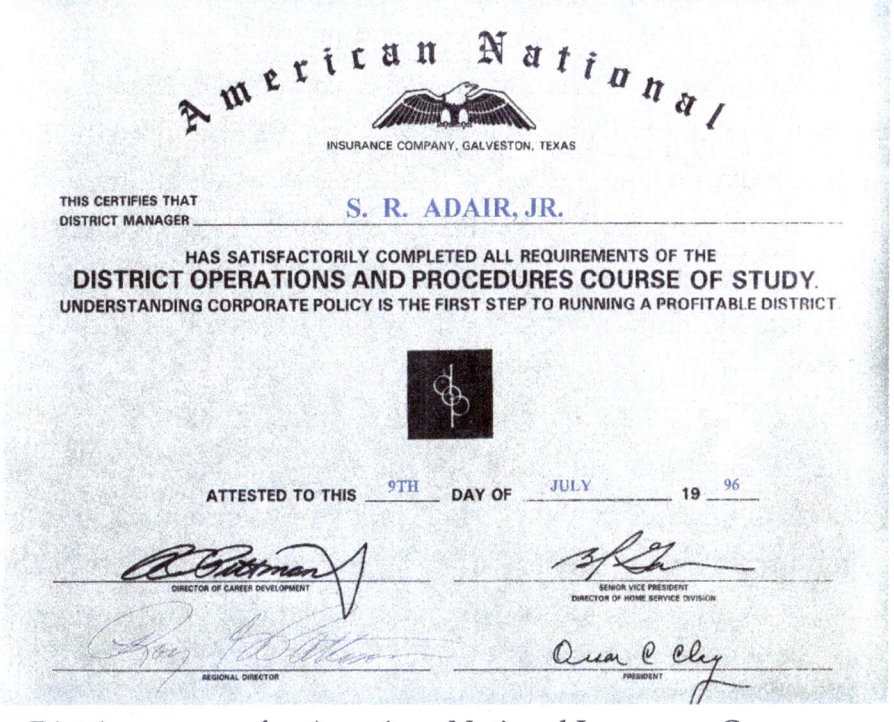

Distric manager for American National Insurance Company

This debit assignment means keeping up with the needs of these clients. Example, making a change of beneficiary, change of address, adding insurance to families as needed due to marriage, child birth, job change, up-grade, helping with a death claim, or other situations and needs.

If some other agent with this same company should write an insurance policy in some other "debit", that sales commission goes to the agent assigned to that debit. The sales Rep. needs to live in that debit area assigned to them. BJ and I live over 100 miles North. For that reason I had to rent a place in the area of Henderson. The apartment we chose was up stairs and in a better part of Henderson. The week would fly by with my work. It kept me busy with getting to know the folks, and helping with their insurance needs.

When the week-end came, it was time to head North, and go home to BJ with our family of geese. Of course there was also Solo, our dog that we both loved so dearly. Once in a while, BJ would make arrangements for her brother to watch the home front, while she came to spend a few days with me. We made this job work, because we wanted to. BJ and I liked to do things together. My church time was always back home at Mt. Olive Baptist, and working with our youth group every Sunday.

(See A.N.D.E. Volume 2 for details.)

American National had an opening for an agent in their Mt. Pleasant Office. That was just 30 miles from our home. It was company policy for agents to transfer to another Agency with the District Manager's approval. My problem was Mr. Weeks, refused to let me transfer. He knew it was near my home, but did not want to lose me. As a result, I turned in my two week notice to leave American National Ins.

Mr. Patterson the Regional Director in Houston called me and hired me back. He wanted me to work in the Mt. Pleasant District

Office as Manager.

Working with the agents here, came with more challenges. I really liked the company a lot, because it covered much of our USA. I had a cousin that worked for them in Baltimore, Md., before she moved to Texas. She transferred to the corporate office in Galveston. There, she met a fellow, married, and still lives in that area. Our area Supervisor was Mr. Bob Patterson from Houston. He was another "kindred spirit". Straight as an arrow, honest, helpful, very supportive and loyal to the customers, agents and company. Our office in Mt. Pleasant, TX had been suffering for more than a year with some bad blood or agents not working in the best interest of the public and the company. My expression is, "you shoot yourself in the foot", when you're not doing your best and refuse to do what is honest and right for all concerned. Mr. Patterson said "Mr. Adair, I'm putting you in charge of a sinking ship. Quite frankly, I do not see any way you can stop the sinking or turn the situation around, but, BEST OF LUCK!" The work was so overwhelming with unfinished claims, etc. Just to mention a few, one policy holder was a nurse. She worked at the hospital in Mt Pleasant, and her husband died of cancer. He had a cancer policy with us but it only paid a small amount in benefits, the wife, (nurse) told me. I took some basic information and looked into that claim for her. Come to find out, the claim had not been processed properly because the field agent had not followed up on some more needed information.

I got Mr. Patterson to help me get this additional information to corporate. He went with me to deliver the balance of that insurance claim. We gave her a check for almost $ 10,000.00, with our most sincere apologies. We were five or six agents short and a lot of work to do. I worked on solving problems full time and did the work of several agents. My income was very steady. I had a good sales record and was very service minded.

I worked to help our customers that had been neglected for so long. That was a hard and tedious job for about a year. The company did close the offices in Mt. Pleasant and in Shreveport, LA, at the same time. All of us that were still working in these two offices were to report to and work out of the office in Marshall, TX. This made for a long commute from home to office and back to our respective work areas, but we did it because it was the right thing to do.

After a while several agents were "let go" and that did not seem right. We knew there were three in this office, that were causing problems. They were still "here", while some good agents were let go, fired or dismissed. When I came in one day, I was given "notice", that my services were no longer needed. "Fired", so I also left. I felt betrayed, I had been lied to by these three "no goods". I knew the home office did not have the true facts about their Marshall Office. Driving straight from Marshall to Galveston, HQ., I called Mr. Patterson. He told me that I would not be able to see the President of ANICO because he was out of town on business. He said he would look into the situation.

When I called my long-time best friend, Mr. Dave Smith at CXI, he asked me to meet him at his TEXMARK office. We had a good visit. His advice was not to be a whistle blower. To just walk away and leave it in the hands of the Good Lord. The news media would have a field day with "my story", as I explained just some of "the TRUTH" to friend Dave. Of course, he was right, the public did not need to be given privileged information on the wrong doings of a few selfish employees, just to keep "my job". About a week later, I received an apology from ANICO. They wanted me to come back to work. I thanked them for the offer and told them Ron Adair would not be back.

AFLAC Insurance Sales

Job # 31, 03/98 to 04/99 AFLAC Insurance, East Texas

This insurance company is by far the finest in the industry, in my opinion. The Home Office Support, as we call them in the field, is top shelf. They do such a great job of giving support. They will do whatever research they can right now when you are on the phone, in a policy holders office, or home, to give them answers needed for peace of mind.

AFLAC Sales Champion

The company policy, is to get the claim one day and have payment in the mail the very next day. In Kilgore, Accurate Machine Co. was a father and son owned business. We knew each other, and they bought AFLAC policies from me. The weekend after their trust in getting AFLAC, the son got a major cut from his elbow to his wrist. That accident required many stitches, and his being disabled for a period of time. This happened on a Saturday, and they called me to ask if this situation was covered by the Ins. they just signed up for. With a few of the details, I called our office and was assured that a check was in the mail as we speak. It was, and they could not believe the prompt service. That check was received on Tuesday, less than a week from taking the coverage. That is just incredible, and I salute the company for doing what needs to be done so professionally.

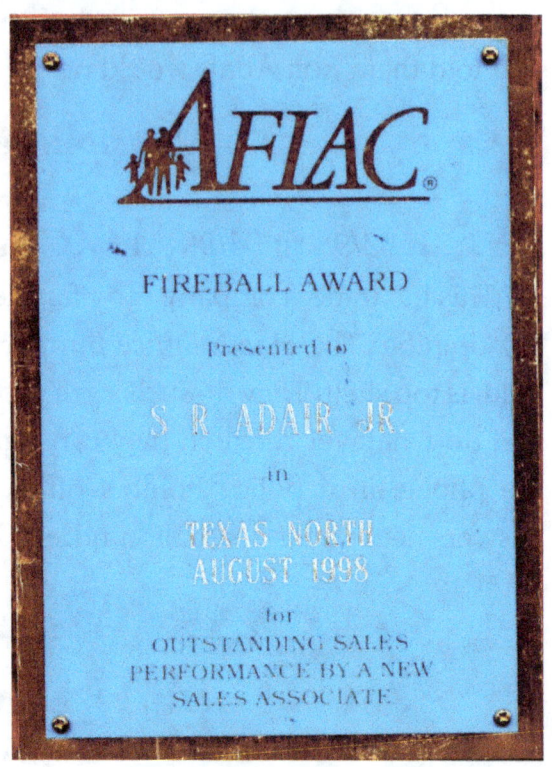

AFLAC sales award

They have a duck for advertising, but believe you me, there is "NO QUACK" anywhere else in this AMERICAN FAMILY LIFE ASSURANCE COMPANY of COLUMBUS (Aflac)

CXI Consultant

Job # 32, 02/98-07/01 CXI / Houston, TX

Sales Consultant and Manufacturing of Bells, among other duties and responsibilities to and for Mr. Smith. It is just another work period in my life when I was available and Dave had a need. It has always worked out and always will, depending on our faith, constant looking ahead and trusting our Lord to walk with us. Have you had days God wasn't close? I have, but guess who moved? Our Lord is always there even in times we feel hurt or let down. He allows us to go through trying times to give us the courage and strength to endure this PROBLEM and the next. He never gives up on us and we should persevere through it all. The Son will shine again. Thank You Lord.

Another Divorce

08/88-07/01 Beginning and End, but still friends.

Another not so good memory, is the end of my second marriage as BJ and I divorced. That was May 10, 2001, we had thirteen very good years together, and even today she will tell you we are good friends and keep in touch by phone every month. Life happens folks, when lemons come your way, and they will, MAKE LEMONADE.

Bettie Jane Nelson is still one of my best friends. We call each other every month, and I will drive to buy her lunch several times every year. We were married for almost thirteen years. She will always be a very special person in my life. While we were married, she lost her Mother, Father, one brother, one sister, and one by one, Solo, and all twelve of our geese, and me. These were all great losses to us both.

FYI, what we did not lose are the precious memories of them all. Every life matters, and the relationships that are built in our life time will touch many lives. BJ and I shared fond memories while working with the Gideons, churches, insurance and various jobs, neighbors, and many friends in many places.

Another Song

These are a few of my favorites: (FYI)

Francis Scott Key... The Start-Spangled Banner;

Doris Akers... Sweet, Sweet, Spirit;

E. M. Bartlett... Victory In Jesus

Albert E. Brumley... I'll Fly Away; Jesus, Hold My Hand; The Blood That Stained the Old Rugged Cross;

Ralph Carmichael... The Savior Is Waiting

R. Kelso Carter... Standing On The Promises

Fanny J. Crosby... Blessed Assurance; Rescue The Perishing; Jesus Is Calling; To God Be The Glory;

John B. Dykes... Holy, Holy, Holy

Edwin O. Excell... Count Your Blessings

William J. Gaither... Because He Lives; He Touched Me; The King Is Coming; The Family Of God;

Stuart Hamblen... It Is No Secret

Stuart K. Hine... How Great Thou Art

Mylon R. LeFevre... Without Him

Mosie Lister... How Long Has It Been;

C. Austin Miles... A New Name In Glory; Dwelling In Beulah Land

John Newton... Amazing Grace

Dottie Rambo... Sheltered In The Arms Of God;

Katharine Lee Bates… America, the Beautiful;

William J. Marsh and Gladys Yoakum Wright… Texas our Texas;

American folk song; The Yellow Rose of Texas

Isaac Watts... Joy To The World;

We're Marching To Zion; & Acres Of Diamonds

Paul Mauriat… Love Is Blue

Thank you for not taking the "option", to stop reading. Remember, "Enjoy Life, This Is Not A Rehearsal".

www.ingramcontent.com/pod-product-compliance
Lightning Source LLC
Chambersburg PA
CBHW071436080526
44587CB00014B/1875